*Celebrating 60 Years*

# The Briar Club
"... For the Purpose of Innocent Sports"

## Celebrating 60 Years

Text by **Nora Seton**

# Dedication

This book is dedicated to the original founding members of The Briar Club.

We remember them for their foresight, their generous spirits, and their legacy.

**Book Committee**

Belle & Peter Petkas – co-chairs
Holland Geibel – professional photographer & graphic artist
Jay Grubb – twice former Club president
Mary Hill – current Board member
John Neighbors – former Club president
Joseph Santamaria – nephew of original owner of property, former Board member
Nora Seton – published author

Houston Public Library's Metropolitan Research Center was invaluable in helping to locate old materials.

**Support Staff**

Richard Lareau – general manager/chief operating officer
Diana Glades – assistant to the general manager
Elizabeth Griffin – membership director
Steve Seyler – property manager

Copyright © 2009 by The Briar Club

All rights reserved, including the right to reproduce this work in any form whatsoever without permission in writing from the publisher, except for brief passages in connection with a review. For information, please write:

The Donning Company Publishers
184 Business Park Drive, Suite 206
Virginia Beach, VA 23462

Steve Mull, General Manager
Barbara Buchanan, Office Manager
Heather L. Floyd, Editor
Lori Wiley, Graphic Designer
Derek Eley, Imaging Artist
Cindy Smith, Project Research Coordinator
Tonya Hannink, Marketing Specialist
Pamela Engelhard, Marketing Advisor

Ed Williams, Project Director

Cataloging-in-Publication Data

Seton, Nora Janssen.
  The Briar Club-- for the purpose of innocent sports : celebrating 60 years / by Nora Seton.
    p. cm.
  ISBN 978-1-57864-566-4 (hardcover : alk. paper)
 1. Briar Club (Houston, Tex.)--History 2. Athletic clubs--Texas--Houston--History. 3. Country clubs--Texas--Houston--History. I. Title.
  GV584.5.T49 2009
  796.0609764'1411--dc22
                          2009012292

Printed in the United States of America at Walsworth Publishing Company

# Contents

*Belle Petkas in "The Dungeon"*

6 / **A Letter from the Presidents, Past and Present**

7 / **A Letter from the General Manager**

8 / **Introduction — The 1940s**

12 / **Chapter 1 — The 1950s**

18 / **Chapter 2 — The 1960s**

26 / **Chapter 3 — The 1970s**

42 / **Chapter 4 — The 1980s**

60 / **Chapter 5 — The 1990s**

68 / **Chapter 6 — The 2000s**

88 / **Our Staff**

92 / **Epilogue**

94 / **Past Presidents**

95 / **Past Briar Ladies Presidents**

96 / **Contributors to Book or Archives**

## *A Letter from the Presidents, Past and Present*

# THE BRIAR CLUB

2603 TIMMONS LANE • HOUSTON, TEXAS 77027 • 713/622-3667 • FAX 713/622-1366

Dear Briar Club Members, Families and Friends,

We are pleased and honored to present this book detailing the wonderful history of our Club. Few institutions can boast of achieving 60 years of history. However, the members who have been a part of The Briar Club over these past years or decades have worked together to make the Club the outstanding institution that it is today.

Whether you swim, play tennis, participate in group exercise, personal training or simply enjoy coming to the Club to meet and relax with your friends and neighbors, The Briar Club has built a reputation as a comfortable sanctuary where families can focus on fun while enjoying excellence in all endeavors.

We members treasure the friendships made and have shared milestone events in our families' histories here. Our Club is a "home away from home" for all our members.

All of this has been brought about by the dedication and active participation of our members, aided by a sensational support staff. The pages of this book and the photos contained inside touch the highlights of our history. It serves as a tribute to all—members and staff—who have been a part of this remarkable community we call The Briar Club.

We hope you enjoy paging through this book as much as we have. It is offered as a tribute to each individual who has participated in our unique history. Happy 60th anniversary!

Sincerely,
Past Presidents

*Standing from left: John Neighbors, Tom Gillette, Peyton Burch, Jeff Cross, Nancy Pustka, Cletus Dodd, Mike Caswell, Jay Grubb, and Ray Frierson.*

*Seated: Mark Worscheh, Bill Wade (current president), and Paige Hagle.*

*Not Pictured: Fred Morgan, Fred Carpenter, Wayne Bardwell, Lee Hancock, Bill Evans, Fisher Trigg, Burke Windham, and Clay Lilienstern.*

## A Letter from the General Manager

# THE BRIAR CLUB
2603 TIMMONS LANE • HOUSTON, TEXAS 77027 • 713/622-3667 • FAX 713/622-1366

Happy sixtieth birthday to The Briar Club. I'm not sure if the quote reads "You don't know"—or "You can't appreciate"—"where you are going unless you know where you have been," but in regard to The Briar Club, both are relevant. To be in the position of chief operating officer of this notable Club carries a heavy responsibility as the guardian of the core values that originally bound our nine founding members together, the vision they shared motivating them to act, and the heritage that has been passed along through their spouses, siblings, and friends on to their children and grandchildren, which has now hardened as the bedrock of our Club's cultural foundation. The Briar Club is more than just a location; it is an idea, a vision of a place that nurtures the soul of our families, and is now multigenerational. This book is a testament to that founding vision. The Club's charter reads that on the 28th day of December 1949, our founding members formed a corporation to be known as The Briar Club, organized "for the purpose of innocent sports."

The pages and pictures that follow are a chronicle of the Club's storied past and illustrate its purpose. Why publish this story now? We are approaching the end of the first decade of this new millennium. The world around us is changing. We have a wonderful opportunity to ensure that our current membership is aware of and understands the "whys" of what exists today. It is only with this understanding that we can progress thoughtfully while preserving and weaving the core values and culture of our past into the fabric of our future, enabling everyone to participate in the process as we move forward. By reading further, you will understand the meaning of the Club's purpose statement and thus the book's title. The story is organized by decade and presented mostly in the words of our members.

This book bears witness to The Briar Club's employees, who for six decades have kept sacred the culture of the community with grace and brightness.

A short number of years ago, with the assistance of the then Board of Directors, a Club mission statement was adopted. The vision, values, and culture depicted in this book are reflected in the mission statement. It is my hope that today's members will come to understand the Club's history, embrace the special culture of its community, and help us extend its vision into the future.

### Mission Statement
*"The Briar Club is a member-owned recreational and social club where a community of families and individuals enjoy the highest standards in aquatics, fitness, tennis, children's programs, and quality cuisine. All programs are presented in attractive surroundings and a comfortable atmosphere, with superior service provided by a highly competent professional staff."*

At Your Service,

*Richard A. Lareau*

Richard A. Lareau, CCM
General Manager/COO

# Introduction

**Houston Chronicle, 1937**

Up to about two years ago, motorists driving west on Westheimer Road noticed an old frame two-story house that stood at the bend in the road just beyond River Oaks. With sagging walls and windows that gaped grotesquely, it was nothing more than a spent shack for the wind to howl through and perhaps a background for a poster or two. In very dim faded letters there stood out something about "Loving Canada" on the side of the old barn-like structure.

Loving Canada is the name of the settlement where about 60 negro families make their homes and do a bit of truck farming for a living…

# The 1940s

The story of the Houston subdivision called Loving Canada began with I. S. Campbell, a black slave who lived in Tennessee in the days before the Civil War. He escaped to Canada where, as luck would have it, a compassionate family took him in. Campbell became educated there and went on to study for the ministry. When the Civil War was over, he was hired to do missionary work in Texas.

Campbell moved first to Galveston, then to Houston, where he settled in the Saint Street area. In 1869, he organized a small church along that bit of road. Many years later, it was re-named the Loving Canada Baptist Church in honor of this old black man, whose stories of a benevolent Canada became renowned from porch to porch. The black settlement along Saint Street was known as the Loving Canada Baptist Church Settlement, and Loving Canada became the name of the subdivision in which The Briar Club stood.

*Tom Gillette: Back about twenty years ago, my brother-in-law bought a lot in the last remaining segment of Loving Canada. This comprised a group of shotgun houses, a residual clump from the original subdivision. They stood between West Alabama and Richmond, on Alabama Court, a tiny street which sneaks off the main road. There were maybe twenty to thirty houses left called Loving Canada in 1980.*

*Loving Canada was the site on which the Coral Club was first established. The Club was considered a "shady lady" kind of place, where you might buy liquor by the glass, dine, dance, and even gamble. It stood in a virtual no-man's land, so remote from Houston's center that it was sometimes difficult to find a police officer. It was surrounded by black settlements, turkey farms, and meadow. West Alabama was a shell road. Buffalo Speedway was a ribbon of gravel. And Saint Street was a collection of shotgun houses up on blocks.*

**John Neighbors:** *If you really look into the history of The Briar Club, you will see it started out from a gambling den—the Las Vegas East.*

*Fannie Santamaria*

Joe Santamaria: Fannie Santamaria, my grandmother, deeded the original tract of land on the corner of Westheimer and Timmons to Uncle Vince so he could build the Coral Club. Fannie was the widow of Joe Santamaria (my namesake and grandfather, who died in 1931) and was also a survivor of the 1900 Galveston Storm. Fannie lived in a house at 1719 Westheimer. She was an amazing cook and provided food for the Coral Club. She taught everybody how to make ravioli.

Uncle Vince was our favorite uncle. He was something of a free spirit. I remember tagging along beside him one day at the Coral Club. He had someone in what's now the Golden Room—an artist painting a mural of Italy.

My Uncle Vince ran the place for a couple of years, and then ran it for the fledgling Briar Club for a couple of years.

I'm happy to lend a little "hysterical reference" (to use Jay Grubb's phrase) to this historical undertaking.

*Vincent Santamaria*

*Jeff Cross:* My parents were charter members. Our member number was number seventy-six. There was a small parking lot where the lap pool is now. Some people would park right on the edge of Timmons, by the lattice fence, and we'd watch their cars slip into the drainage ditch.

There were only two tennis courts. We would sometimes hit balls over the fence into where there were rows of houses. We'd have to scramble over to retrieve the balls, and the residents did not like that one bit.

The Golden Room was the original farmhouse. The old offices were upstairs, and the shower stall up there was the storage room for the Bingo cards.

It was a nice Club, kind of exciting around the edges.

In the last days of 1949, Houston prepared for a winter wave. On December 30th, a major metropolitan referendum was scheduled to decide whether to annex seventy-nine square miles of surrounding communities. The annexation was a commitment to Houston's continuous growth. On this same momentous day, thirteen local men, recent veterans of World War II, made concrete plans to improve the lives of their families and many others for years to come. They filed a charter with the state of Texas to recognize The Briar Club. A fee of seventy dollars was paid. The following morning, Houstonians woke up to discover they lived in the South's most populous city.

Gerald E. Veltmann (from an oral history dictated to and transcribed by Virginia Barry in 1982): After World War II, about twelve or thirteen of us needed a place for pleasure and enjoyment with our families—a place that was not too expensive. We had a number of children in our households and no place to swim or play tennis. We decided we would try to organize a Club, and we lucked into a facility. The address was 3637 Westheimer, facing on Timmons Lane. It was owned by one Vincent Santamaria.

Vincent had a brother who was a lawyer here in Houston, and a mother who was an exceptional cook. She was the chef for what was then known as the Coral Club, a private club owned by her son Vincent. The Coral Club was without a swimming pool or tennis courts, but with good Italian food as a private Club, and a substantial bar and game rooms, which provided pleasure to the members of that Club.

This was in the early part of 1949, and it wasn't too long after the Coral Club was going that three fine-looking young men came into the Club. They impressed Vincent Santamaria to such an extent that he offered to sell them a drink. Unfortunately for Vincent, these three young men were agents of the Texas State Liquor Control Board, and it was not a few days later that the padlock was put on the Coral Club.

The twelve or thirteen of us who started trying to find Club facilities for our families were referred to as the "dirty dozen," or sometimes the "baker's dozen." We made contact with Vincent, who was really quite receptive to our proposal that we take on a new Club.

On the property stood the one old building. Inside were a ballroom, a dining room, and a reception area, where there was a raised brick fireplace with an imposing copper hood above it. The back room had a bar and cocktail lounge, all of it most notable because of the very dark interior, which was probably designed to provide greater… relaxation. The old kitchen was in the approximate position of the 1982-era Briar Club kitchen, although now many times expanded. There were also two rooms upstairs.

We struck a deal with Vincent agreeing that he would have the exclusive food purveying privilege so long as 51 percent of the membership approved his food ingredients and service. We negotiated a lease for five years with an option to purchase at any time during that period, and as I recall, a right to renew for an additional five years should we remain as lessees for that five-year period of time. Incidentally, we exercised that option to purchase approximately one year after the Club was organized.

In order to execute a valid lease with Vincent, we needed a corporation, and under the date of December 28, 1949, I prepared a charter for the then expected-to-be Briar Club. The charter was signed by the original nine directors, who were Winthrop W. Carter III, Warren P. Cunningham, Jr., Kraft W. Eidman, Louis M. LeMaster, U. D. Porter, Miles M. Strickland, Herbert W. Varner, John C. Williams, and myself. I drafted the charter in the law offices of the firm of which I was then associated, and the wife of the senior member of our firm, named Naomi Guinn, was notary public. She acknowledged the signatures of all nine of us who signed as the original directors.

Herbert Varner, who was one of the original directors, claims to have won the contest, which we had in the early stages of the negotiation, for a new name. The word *Briar*, spelled with an *a*, alluded to the number of brier bushes that were on the property—particularly behind and around the Clubhouse.

Warren P. Cunningham, Jr. was our first president. At the first formal meeting, when we had Vincent Santamaria present to sign and acknowledge the lease, his brother Foley showed up and started claiming that we had mistreated his brother Vincent, and that he thought he would file a lawsuit to stop all negotiations. Then Foley looked around and saw many of his legal colleagues present, and he decided that might not be prudent.

It was in early January that construction, which was required by the lease-purchase agreement, began under the supervision of Vincent Santamaria. The construction included what is now the Plantation Room, which housed new offices. What I have referred to as the Plantation Room was known as the Venetian Room for many years and has recently been renamed the Briar Room. The westerly wing of the property embraced the swimming pool and the tennis courts, the pool filtering room, and the locker rooms for men and women, as well as new offices for the manager, his assistants, and staff.

## Chapter 1

```
           BRIAR CLUB SPECIAL BULLETIN
                BRIAR    LADIES
           STYLE  SHOW  LUNCHEON
               "PRELUDE TO FALL"
             Fashions By Wolfman's
           By Our Own Lovely Models
       MAKE UP A PARTY            GUESTS WELCOME
              WEDNESDAY, OCTOBER 21ST, 1959
       COME IN FOR COCKTAILS 11:30 PM   LUNCHEON at 12:30 PM
                                              $2.25
                  STYLE SHOW 1:30 PM
                 - - - - -*- - - - -

                     FAMILY NITE
              THURSDAY, OCTOBER 22ND
                       BUFFET DINNER 6 'til 8 PM
       CASH PRIZES               RESERVATIONS PLEASE!
                 - - - - -*- - - - -

       ON THE HOUSE   OYSTER BAR - EVERY FRIDAY
                          6 'til 8 PM
                 - - - - -*- - - - -

                  BREAKFAST   DANCE
               SATURDAY, OCTOBER 24TH
          DANCE TO THE MUSIC OF AL MARKS' ORCHESTRA
                       9 'til 1
             RESERVATIONS            JA 3-7456
                 - - - - -*- - - - -
       HAVE YOU
               Tried our Superb Sunday Evening Buffet Dinner?
                       VERY POPULAR!
```

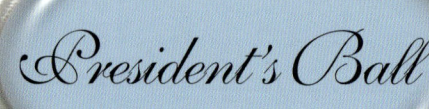

President's Ball

# The 1950s

```
                SPECIAL        BULLETIN

        GREAT ENTERTAINMENT AT THE BRIAR CLUB
    Thursday TUESDAY, JUNE 25TH   1959
            CHUCK CABOT'S ORCHESTRA WITH THE
                    "INK SPOTS"
    LAST NOTICE * AT THIS TIME RESERVATIONS ARE NEARLY FILLED
    RESERVE NOW - - BREAKFAST AND DANCE $4.00 - SEMI-FORMAL
    IF YOUR RESERVATIONS HAVE BEEN MADE, PLEASE DOUBLE CHECK
                    * * * * * * *
            FAMILY NITE BUFFET DINNER EVERY THURSDAY
            ( EXCEPT THURSDAY, JUNE 25TH)
            RECENT BIG WINNER, MRS. JEFFERSON GILLER, $200.00
                    * * * * * * *
            TEEN AGE JUKE BOX DANCE & SWIMMING PARTY
                SATURDAY, JUNE 20TH - 8 PM 'TIL 11 PM

            BRIAR PATCHERS JUKE BOX DANCE & SWIMMING PARTY
                FRIDAY, JUNE 26TH - 7PM 'TIL 10 PM
            NO GUEST CHARGE ON TEENAGE OR BRIARPATCHERS
                            REFRESHMENTS
                    * * * * * * * * * * * * *
```

**PRESIDENTS**
1950 Warren P. Cunningham, Jr.
1951 Gerald E. Veltmann
1952 Kraft W. Eidman
1953 Ed A. Smith
1954 John C. Williams
1955 W. Kenneth Davis
1956 Dr. J. M. Dougall
1957 Shelton W. Boyce, Jr.
1958 Zeke Tipton
1959 Zeke Tipton

Presidents Harry Truman and Dwight Eisenhower led America into the 1950s as the warcraft industries of the 1940s were converted into peacetime production for a booming America. In 1953, Houston's KUHT put the nation's first public broadcast television station on the air. The metropolitan population reached and topped one million. In 1955, Rosa Parks refused to give up her seat on a bus in Montgomery, Alabama, to a white passenger. Jonas Salk created a vaccine against polio. Alaska and Hawaii became the forty-ninth and fiftieth states in 1959.

Houston flourished in this decade of industrial growth. The city was also a go-to source for rubber, aluminum, and chemicals, which became critical during the Korean conflict.

During the 1950s, The Briar Club as we now know it truly began to take shape. The first pool was built. An initial code of conduct was established, which included a dress code for members and guests. Monthly dues were instituted, as well as a check system for the purchase of food and beverages. A membership fee of three hundred dollars plus 20 percent tax was charged. Furniture for the cocktail lounge was purchased from Suniland Furniture. In 1956, Al Chivers was hired as manager, remaining in that position for over twenty-five years.

The Briar Ladies organized and kicked off with a Box Supper. The purpose of the Briar Ladies was to raise funds for a program to improve and beautify the Club. They arranged monthly meetings with a speaker or entertainer. The dues were annual, tacked onto the Briar Club bill, on top of which the ladies then paid for their lunches.

Not to be outdone, the children of The Briar Club also organized very active clubs. During these years, the Briar Patchers, aged ten to twelve years old, were known to have platter parties. The Briarteens, at thirteen to fifteen years old, held many swimming parties (eighty-five cents per person). The Junior Board, whose members where sixteen to twenty years old, enjoyed several informal dances (seventy-five cents per person).

Club events were very well attended. The Briar Night Committee gave away mink stoles, all-expense-paid trips to Mexico City, and color television sets. Busses were chartered to take fans to college football games. Chef Gene Caler created Gourmet Sunday Buffets, which became famous throughout Houston.

Gerald E. Veltmann: In those days, you drank your own liquors, which had to be taken to the Club and put into your personal locker. This was required under the law. The locker arrangement worked as a matter of practice, except that on every Saturday night when we had a dance with live music—over-subscribed in every instance—the bartender got so busy that he'd grab the first bottle he could get his hands on to fix a drink for anyone who came up and asked. As a result, if your bottle happened to be on the first row, the next time you went to the Briar Club with a guest for dinner or lunch and asked for a drink, expecting your own portions still intact, you might find yourself without liquor.

Ultimately we were able, as a private Club, and under the supervision of the Liquor Control Board, to avoid the locker system, and it became much more convenient and the service much better when libations were desired.

We also had a manager, after the one mentioned earlier, who applied to the Club carrying *The Saturday Evening Post* and newspaper clippings testifying to his proficiency as a Club manager at several other outstanding private Clubs, including one in Honolulu, Hawaii.

He was small, neat, and well-dressed, and assured us on interview that he had no interest in consuming liquors of any type, and expected that he would provide exceptional service to the Club. We hired him. And this gentleman—and he was that—who was also noted as a professor at Vassar College some years before, continued to appear for his duties at The Briar Club in a morning coat and striped trousers with the greatest flair that you can imagine. We felt we had stumbled upon a gem, and did not take the time to check his references.

Well, one of our original directors, Louis M. LeMaster, had been a member of the FBI. His inquisitiveness drew attention to our foolishness when, without any comment to the other members of the Board, he wrote letters to the noted references in the employment application of this manager. As only could be expected, every reference replied that they had never heard of the gentleman. Incidentally, he was the man who first installed the chit system at The Briar Club for the purchase of drinks, rather than the exchange of cash or signing of checks.

In desperation, we happened to hear that Grover C. Johnson had retired as the general manager of the River Oaks Country Club. I made a beeline with Warren Cunningham and a couple of others to visit with Mr. Johnson and convince him that he needed The Briar Club to fill his empty days, and that we needed him as our manager over on Westheimer. Mr. Johnson accepted the position. He found a chef known as

John Hall, who stayed with The Briar Club for many years and became a subsequent manager. I might mention that he should have stayed in the kitchen. He later went to the Hobby Airport as chef at the old Hobby Terminal Building and did well as a chef.

Mr. Johnson was our Santa Claus, and because of his stature, was fondly referred to by that name. He was always at the front door with a jolly, pleasant word for everyone who came into The Briar Club. The children were most fond of him. During my tenure as president, Flager Tannery, the comptroller of Humble Oil & Refining Company, was our treasurer. It was then we discovered that Mr. Johnson did everything *except* manage the Club. However, he was worth every nickel or dollar that was paid to him, and he created an atmosphere at the Club which has not been excelled to this day.

For the commencement of swimming season on San Jacinto Day of 1950, the new pool was ready to be emptied and cleaned. We planned a formal dedication of the pool and Club facilities at that time. The contractor put a pump on the side of the pool, put a hose deep into the deep end of the pool, and put the outgoing hose into what appeared to be a storm sewer opening. The pool was about half-filled with water and had no water escape-valves in the bottom, which I understand were used to be sure that the pool stayed in position when the water was out. As a result, instead of the water being pumped into an open storm sewer, the water was being pumped underneath the new swimming pool. Finally, as the water was under the pool in great abundance, the pool popped up like a cork about eighteen inches from where it had been securely seated. This was only about two or three days before San Jacinto Day and it happened late evening. The workmen found out about it the next morning and we didn't know whether we were going to have an opening or not. However, the pool was finally emptied and then filled so that the weight of the water in the pool started settling it back into its original hole.

On San Jacinto Day, the pool did open and we put bricks up around the side. It was probably not more than six or eight inches higher than where we intended the pool to be in the first place. It did hold water and it did not crack which, of course, was very fortunate. That was the beginning of funny things at The Briar Club.

The lounge was a small, dark room which had a curved *S*-type mahogany bar used during the Coral Club days. There were probably two or three tables and chairs in the dimly lit cocktail area. Ultimately, we extended the room south. Since the *S*-curved bar took up three times as much as was needed, the bar was moved along the west wall. What is now the bar and cocktail area was still quite misused and certainly not very attractive.

One of our members and a director at one time, Graham Mallet, worked for the Graham Paper Company. He commented to me that they had some grass cloth paper which could be put across the front of the rather beat-up bar without a great deal of trouble and with just some few tacks and staples. We conspired to redecorate the front of the bar with this grass cloth material whenever Graham might be able to bring some from his mill.

We did so one morning shortly thereafter at about eleven or eleven-thirty in the morning. Graham and I were busily engaged, and we were making substantial progress into getting the front of the bar to look quite presentable, when some of the ladies who were playing bridge in the new cocktail lounge area sent the

*Standing in front of the cocktail lounge at Easter time are Gay Veltmann (Conner) and Carol Cox (Ferguson).*

manager over and said to get those two workmen out of the Club while they were having their bridge play. Graham and I sort of tittered, got through as quickly as we could, and got the hell out of there.

The Briar Club members really did enjoy our Club activities. It wasn't a matter of having a dance once a quarter or once every six months. It practically boiled down to having a dance with live music nearly every weekend. Reservations flowed in very promptly when a notice was sent out about a dance party, usually with a buffet, and that attendance continued right along for a number of years. We had two tennis courts which were blacktop. We had a very suitable swimming pool, and we had a wading pool for children. We finally avoided the locker system for liquor bottles and all in all had a most enjoyable group.

I can tell you that instead of holding one Board of Directors meeting each month, for a long time we had at least one meeting every week, and sometimes two while we were trying to solve the problem of management. We would start a meeting at seven and quite frequently get home at two in the morning.

We found that we were able to do much of the maintenance and upkeep in and around the Club through member participation. These were things that otherwise would have cost substantial sums. I have in mind particularly our painting the entire inside of The Briar Club, upstairs and downstairs, on one Thanksgiving Day, when Texas and Texas A&M were playing college football at College Station. This was in November 1951, and members had been invited by letter to appear at seven or so on that Thanksgiving morning with a three-inch paintbrush. We assured them that high-quality paint would be available as well as cold lunch and kegs of beer, with a radio giving us the returns of the football game throughout the Club property. I can't remember the exact number that showed up, but there were far too many, and each person with a three-inch brush could have probably painted his part in a matter of one to two hours.

Bob West and his brother-in-law, Jim Littler, and their wives showed up with six-inch paint rollers. We didn't know exactly what to do with them so we assigned them the entire upstairs. With the ladies holding the paint trays, and Bob and Jim Littler rolling the paint on with those brushes, they were probably through in forty-five minutes. Realizing the speed with which they could paint, we soon recruited them for the downstairs. We finished the job at about four-thirty on Thanksgiving afternoon. The football game was coming to an end and the beer tubs or kegs were empty.

I forgot to mention that I got the paint at a wholesale price from a neighbor who lived on the block near me. He was also a member of the Club.

---

*John Neighbors: Before 1949, the Club was operating without the benefit of legality. It was just a bunch of guys getting together and playing poker and having a drink or two. This was the old Santamaria farm. The building that was here… it was an old farmhouse. That's what they made into the Coral Club.*

*Texas in those days did not allow open bars, so there was a regular brown bag rule. You could not have an open bottle unconcealed. Private clubs could set up lockers for each member, and you could put your bottle in your personal locker. When you wanted a drink, the bartender would take your bottle to the bar and pour you a drink. A locker was big enough to hold two bottles—two fifths. Each had a little plate and a little number.*

*Well, the storage at The Briar Club was all in one room, about where the membership office is now. It was a big closet, and it was called Locker 500, and I'll bet there were over five hundred bottles in there.*

Al Chivers: When I joined The Briar Club as manager, it was in its infancy. The pool was very narrow, elongated, probably thirty by one hundred feet. It had a surround made out of lattice. You could see it from the street, and the only thing that separated it from the street was the ditch that ran down Timmons. The lanai—this outer building—wasn't there. Everything was close to the street. The Club had a narrow lot.

In those days, Westheimer was two lanes without an esplanade. If you swerved off the shoulder you slid down into a culvert and had to wait for a tow truck. Timmons had ditches at that time, where the sidewalks are now. Well, people on the Board of the Club were also on the School Board, and they didn't want their Club to be in a mud hole. So it was only a matter of time before the city paved the street.

That swimming pool was full from sun-up to sundown. And let me tell you, the kids that played in the Briar Club pools have gone on to become real icons.

Al Chivers: In the fifties, The Briar Club had steam cabinets. These closed up around your neck, steamed you up. Steam cabinets and A/C made this Club pop. Before I came on as manager, there was supposedly a single bowling alley.

The old pool was built… it was like a reverse chimney. They laid rebar into the desired shape. They lined the outside with wood, and then they built the inside trough from wood. They went down into the hole to complete the shape, and then they poured the cement.

It leaked all the time! It had to be plastered continuously. They tried to wait until October to plaster. You're covering up the leaks and the holes with some grout and then bleaching it so it looks good. Mostly we tried to control the chemicals, and we probably overdid that. The chlorides were too strong; people's eyes were burning. We didn't have good chemicals then.

Al Chivers: Howard Lee was an oilman who was married to Hedy Lamarr. They lived on Del Monte and this was in the fifties. She used to come over here. In the fifties, one-piece bathing suits were pretty much the order of the Club. I happened to be at their house one day, and their daughter, Toni, came down the stairs, and mind you I'd never seen this kind of thing. She comes down the stairs in this two-piece bathing suit. It was unbelievable—a bikini! I'd never seen one. And my mouth fell open. And she said, "Would this be welcome over at the Club?"

And I said, "I'd welcome it. I'm not sure… The Briar Club policy has generally been modesty."

The Briar Club has always been like that. It at all times had decorum. What was very entrenched here was a sense of family and faith.

## NOTE OF INTEREST

THE RIVER OAKS ROTARY CLUB RECEIVED ITS' CHARTER AT THE BRIAR CLUB ON OCT. 2, 1959, AND HAS MET HERE EVERY TUESDAY WITH LUNCHEON AT 12:15. MANY OF OUR OWN BRIAR CLUB MEMBERS ARE RIVER OAKS ROTARIANS AND MANY BELONG TO OTHER ROTARY CLUBS. A GREAT NUMBER OF ROTARIANS MAKE UP FOR ATTENDANCE AT THE BRIAR CLUB. THE BRIAR CLUB HAS A RECORD FOR THE BEST FOOD. THIS SHOULD MAKE US ALL PROUD. IF YOU ARE A ROTARIAN, WHY NOT MAKE UP AT THE BRIAR CLUB?

## Chapter 2

# The 1960s

**PRESIDENTS**
| | |
|---|---|
| 1960 | Ira W. Strickler |
| 1961 | J. B. Ross |
| 1962 | J. B. Ross |
| 1963 | Sam Tigner |
| 1964 | Evert A. Rogers |
| 1965 | Robroy C. Carroll |
| 1966 | Joffre J. Cross |
| 1967 | Lewis F. Scherer |
| 1968 | H. E. Carrico, Jr. |
| 1969 | J. F. Freel |

The post-World War II "baby boom" created tens of millions of teenagers in the 1960s. The Woodstock festival collected nearly a half-million "hippies" for a week of music and love-ins. Martin Luther King, Jr., Fidel Castro, and John F. Kennedy launched pivotal social change. In the midst of it all, America entered into the Vietnam War.

In the 1960s, NASA established the "Manned Spacecraft Center" in Houston. It was later renamed the Lyndon B. Johnson Space Center. In 1969, Houston was the first word uttered from the surface of the moon, and the Houston Astrodome, touted as "The Eighth Wonder of the World," opened.

Timmons Lane was paved during these years. The Briar Club formed its first Tennis Committee. The Board of Directors instituted a Junior Membership for the Club. To qualify, the member had to be between the ages of twenty-one and thirty. The Club became a popular lunch spot, catering to over two hundred people per day. Al Chivers set out breakfast service for a group of men that swam each weekend morning.

The Club still operated with "Trustees of Locker 500" who were requested to comply with all directives of the Texas Liquor Control Board. Liquor sold by the drink was still not legal in Texas.

Toward the end of the decade a new parking lot was paved, fenced, and lighted. A twenty-five-meter lap pool was installed where the old parking lot had been, and new practice courts for tennis players were built. In 1968, the Club held its very first Derby Day. It was standing room only.

Jay Grubb: I believe you heard me say that prior to the lap pool, we parked in that space and crawled through the shrubbery to enter the Club proper. There was no room to turn around so we had to back out into Timmons—not as busy as now—but "peligro" in any case, and just as bumpy!

The **SHRIMP BOATS** are in again!!!!!
Friday, June 19
6:30 p.m. till 8:30 p.m.
FOR THE ADULTS: all the Beer You Can Drink
A fish fry, too.... $3.00
And music for your dancing pleasure.

MENU
Iced JUMBO SHRIMP - Fried CATFISH
Cole Slaw, Gumbo, Jambalaya,
Potato Salad, French Bread,
RESERVATIONS, Please!

 **FATHERS DAY**

CELEBRATE FATHERS DAY- JUNE 21st
Bring Father, and Grandfather, to *The Briar Club*.

"A Special Feast"- has been planned
12 noon til 3:00 p.m.; evening, 6:00 til 8:30 p.m.
All of Dad's Favorite Foods will be featured.

Special, Dad only $2.00,     "MITCH" at the Organ
others at regular prices     Reservations JA 3-7456

Al Chivers: The Briar Club had one of the first air-conditioned buildings out this far west. I say "this far" because it was farm and meadow here. Lamar High School went up in 1937 and it was considered "out in the country."

Air conditioning was pretty cutting-edge, but like any new system, there were hitches. There were always leaks in the chillwater. Chillwater used to be a contained system of water moving through a water tower. You had an outside condensing unit in a latticed enclosure. The water tower was made of wood. It looked like a giant closet. Water ran through chillers, then you had a blow-down through a blower. The return air was only in one spot in the building. There was no zoning.

For amenities and comfort, the Club rivaled River Oaks in a lot of ways. The campus here was more relaxed, and people just rolled out of the adjacent residential areas. Lots of kids came on foot, carrying a tennis racquet or swimsuit…

We had a lot of patio parties. For kids, during the day, there was music and there were a lot of food fights. Come evening, you had Club members come in looking for the more adult environment. About four o'clock, the gears shifted, a transitional difference between the cadence of the day and the evening.

Jeff Cross: The Club was pretty popular back in the sixties. We'd have more people here than were at River Oaks. The R.O. kids would come over here. We could get by with more. Mr. Chivers never came out by the pool. He didn't like the poolside; it was hot out there. He stayed indoors. So we'd have a big time out there.

*Jay Grubb: In 1963, some business associates of mine said, "Grubb, we're going to allow you to join the Club at no charge." The Briar Club at that time had an E Membership, which attached to a Corporate Membership. In my case, it was the Union Texas Petroleum Corporation. My number was X-777. Half the company had lunch at the Briar Club every weekday.*

*A few years later, when I found out I was going to run for the Board, I had to buy an Equity Membership. In those days we bought and sold memberships among and between. It didn't go through the Club at all. I bought mine from a Lamar High School classmate that joined River Oaks.*

# The Briar Club launched a monthly publication called *Whispers*.

---

hankerin' fer oysters? Zat what you want, Bunky???
Well, this is just fer yew:

## OYSTER BAR

Served in the cocktail lounge from 7 until 8 on Friday November first. All you can eat for only One Dollar. Naturally the oysters taste better if you have a cocktail or two preceding ordering.

**ALL YOU CAN EAT — $1.00**

---

### 2 Great Sunday Treats

**EVERY SUNDAY**
Meet – Me – After – Church
Buffet Dinner

$1.50 children 4 through 11 years
$2.00 12 years through 16 years
All over 16 years $2.50

No charge for children under 4 years

---

NEW HAS BEEN ADDED
...rs More Beautiful and Healthy

### Sauna Bath

So goes the story:
"One is most beautiful two hours after the Sauna Bath."

You will want to make your appointment for the use of the Sauna Bath to coincide with your Social Calendar. It is ready for use NOW. But, for the time being, you should call the office for an appointment. For any information, call JA 3-7456. Ladies Raid 319.00 balance

---

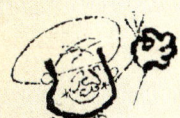

**Friday Shrimp Boat**

### SHRIMP PEEL
**Friday, April 16**

THE SHRIMP BOAT IS IN — Will be poolside weather permit...

**for only $2.75 per person**

this is it — 6:30 till 9:00 p.m.
All the shrimp you can eat — you peel them
Plus other goodies
Seafood Gumbo — Jambalaya
Potato salad — cole slaw — pickles — olives
French bread — peach cobbler
Price does not include... on your own)
...67

---

# WHISPERS at the BRIAR CLUB

Published Monthly          December 1967

## Oyster Gourmet Dinner

**FRIDAY, DECEMBER 22nd — 4.50**

Oysters—Oysters—Oysters—Oysters—Oysters
You Name It We Have It!

**ALL YOU CAN EAT**

| | |
|---|---|
| Oysters on the Half Shell | Oysters a la King |
| Oysters Aspect | Oysters Rockefeller |
| Oysters Kirpatrick | Oyster Gumbo |
| Oysters Biltmore | Oyster Stew |
| Oysters Smoked | Oyster Burgandy |
| Oysters Fried | Creole Shrimp |

This is just a sample of goodies you will enjoy—All YOU can eat for—4.50
**RESERVATIONS NOW — NA 2-3667**

**Briar Club Annual Children's Christmas Party**
1:00 UNTIL 2:30 P.M.

---

*Briar Ladies*

## Buzzin' Round the Briar

Your Club becoming a "Fashion Show" on so many occasions . . . take the 11th of April, Easter Egg Hunt Day, and so many fashionable Missy's and Master's and what personalities, the future members of the BRIAR CLUB . . . among the group on the poolside lawn looking for the colored eggs and mostly the plastic eggs with the winning numbers for the larger prizes of baskets filled with goodies and those lovely plush rabbits in all colors were: Master's Jim and John Douglas, grandchildren of the W. P. Crouch's neatly attired in red and blue plaid Eton jackets, short black pants and red bow ties. . . . Tracie ...bitt like a dream in her ... with a white overskirt ... Cindy in a sleeveless blue empire princess dress carrying a blue basket to match and let's not forget brother Randy in a blue striped beige jacket and short brown pant's, grandchildren of the Robroy Carrol's . . . Ann Johnson, the R. W. Johnson heiress in pink check pinafore with deep white yoke and carrying a frilled white basket . . . Cindy Freel in deep yellow with white collar and Jerry Freel, namesake of grandfather J. F. Freel, in green, blue and white checked Eton jacket with navy short pants . . . Bill O'Donnell and sister Jennifer both in their holiday finery . . . Blake Tartt looking like a southern gentleman in a two piece white pique suit and a shirt with his initials on the collar, HBT . . . the Brinkman children, all six: John, Joe, Fred, Pam, Debbie, and Tricia . . . having as their guest Julie Ann Straub of Kansas City, their niece . . . who wore a sleeveless red smocked pinafore with many white buttons and shoes to match—buttons on them, too . . . Carolyn Strickler came with Momma and Grandmother too, in a white dotted swiss full skirted dress and a wide deep pink sash with a ribbon to match in her long tresses carrying a red feather basket . . . Susan and Frank Burge in brother and sister outfits . . . Tina Armstrong, a lovely blonde with a pony tail in a navy jumper and white blouse . . . Sarah Walker, grandchild of the R. O. Bell's, a picture in her red printed picadilly challis with a matching headscarf . . . Karen and Peyton Crouch dressed in blue . . . Callana and Jean Wright, the idols of the J. Ross Wright's (they are twins) came in blue sailor dresses with matching shorts and white patent slippers and we must not forget Karen Ormstron, the youngest child at the hunt and enjoying it, too, seven weeks old in pink with a blue blanket . . . Winner of the prizes were: Missy Jennifer O'Donnell, Glenda Hail, Kathy Nesbitt, Karen Crouch, Laura Jane Handley, Caroline Strickler, Callana Wright, Martha Hoaglin, Barbara Hoaglin, Kristina Duemer and Master's Jerry Freel, Peyton Crouch, Frankie Burge, Ricky Hail, Bill O'Donnell, Pat Frede, Joe Harris and Dickie Hoaglin . . . See you next month, **Ellie.**

21

The Board authorized the Facilities Committee to try to purchase property facing Timmons and Westheimer (now the location of Whataburger). The owner asked for $3.50 per square foot. This was too expensive for the Club. The Club then tried to purchase the Gay property (east of the tennis courts). The Committee was authorized to pay as much as $2.50 per square foot. The Club badly needed the extra land for parking and expansion.

*Randy Burch: I joined The Briar Club in 1966. I remember exactly where I was sitting at the time; in my office on Kirby Drive. Peyton was eleven.*

*The Briar Club had D Memberships at the time. You could come and use everything but you couldn't vote. That's what we did. Some years later, in 1970, they called and asked me if I wanted to become an A Member. For $250, I became an A Member. Our sponsor was the Club president at that time, Pete Lipscomb.*

*In 1964, a Thanksgiving dinner was served buffet style. The cost was $3.00 for adults, $2.25 for juniors, $1.50 for children, and was free to children under three years of age.*

In January 1965, the petition to pave Timmons Lane was signed by all adjoining property owners. The paving and curbing were completed in 1967.

Briar Ladies Bingo

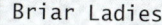

Briar Ladies

Peyton Burch: When you were a little kid and you went to Bingo, you had to wear a coat and tie. You went in there, had your dinner, and it was a quiet, somber atmosphere. That was the culture everywhere then. Children were seen and not heard. You learned how to handle yourself in public by dressing right and keeping quiet. Those were more formal times. The Club used to keep extra coats and ties out there, in case you forgot your own and wanted to dine here.

Bingo was a big anchor-point for The Briar Club. It was called "Briar," not Bingo. You played "Briar." You came for "Briar Night." The cards were printed *BRIAR* across the top. You had to juggle two *R*'s on your card. There was an element of cleverness involved. It was great, great fun.

July 2, 1968 minutes from the Board: To Jere Freel from John Buckley: "I blame the correctness of these minutes on three martinis and a double scotch."

# LUAU

THE LUAU — Saturday, June 19
AT WAIKIKI BEACH (THE BRIAR CLUB)
ON THE ISLAND OF OAHU

## THE LUAU — Saturday, June 19
### AT WAIKIKI BEACH (THE BRIAR CLUB)
### ON THE ISLAND OF OAHU

Okole Maluna 7:00 p.m. til 9:00 p.m. "Ono — Ono Kaukau" 9:00 p.m. The Wahine will wear her Nani Muumuu, the Kane will wear his brightly colored "Aloha shirt or may be dressed picturesquely as a beachcomber." There will be dancing in the Lanai till 1:00 a.m. Mouth watering teriyaka sticks and batter fried shrimp will be served during the cocktail hour before dinner is served.

After the appetites are appeased, the entertainment starts. Musicians will play their lilting rhythms.

The atmosphere at a luau is one of warm congenial friendliness. Old friends indulge in much conversation and gossip — young boys and girls delight in each others company — and the children play harmoniously together. There is much laughter and joy in the air — it is for all ages. This simple gay fun-making is Hawaiian hospitality.

If you do not plan to stay for dancing, we recommend you bring your older children for dinner and entertainment before the dance. They will like dressing like Mom and Dad. Children's prices will be the same as adults. Kala. — $4.50 per person.

This is a promise for a Luau like Houston has never seen before. You must make reservations — NA 2-3667. First reservations to come in will be assigned the choice tables. All tables will be table high (except by special request). It will not be necessary for you to sit on the ground unless by your choice.

Lei (pronounced lay) — perhaps one of the most delightful of Island customs — is that of Lei giving. The gift of a lei symbolizes many emotions: joy, welcome, farewell, a thousand shades of love, and deep comradeship. There are many feelings that one cannot express but one can always drape a Lei around his or her neck.

The traditional and graceful way to give a Lei, "Hawaiian style" is to place the garland gently around the neck of the recipient, accompanying the Lei with a kiss. At parties, the host greets "Wahine" guests and the hostess greets each "Kane" guest with a Lei. It is a warm and friendly prelude to any social occasion.

A Lei may be worn in any manner, as long as it is comfortable to the wearer. Usually that means placing the Lei so that a part of it hangs to the back rather than snugly against the back of the neck. Leis may be worn in any number. These symbols of thoughtfulness and affection are worn happily and proudly.

Ono Ono Luau Kaukau Nani

The word Luau, the traditional island celebration feast conveys a gay and joyous occasion where good fellowship reigns supreme.

It is not necessary to serve unknown foods to a malihini (mah-lee-hee-nee) newcomer or tourist, but menu should include bananas, pineapples, coconuts, sweet potatoes, pork, chicken and salmon. For the Briar Club Kaukau, this menu has been chose, "Haole Style":

Pineapple juice
Baked fish with coconut sauce
Kalua Pig — whole roasted from underground oven
Chicken Hawaiian
Pineapple sticks with coconut cookies
Creamy Bread Pudding (Malinini Pai)
Spring Salad
Sweet-Sour Spare Ribs
Japanese Salad
Lomi Salmon
Sweet Potatoes Hawaiian
Laulaus (tora leaves or spinach)
Kono Coffee

**HOW MANY IN YOUR PARTY FOR THE LUAU? CALL NA 2-3667**

### WHAT TO WEAR

To go native in dress, comfort is the prime requisite, typical luau wear in the islands are muumuus, holomus and holokuus for the wahines, and ⟨fo⟩r the men, multi-colored "aloha" ⟨s⟩hirty, the children emulate their elder counterparts. Little girls look like live dolls dressed in colorful muumuus with fragrant leis and flowers in their hair.

### THE MUUMUU

The muumuu is the straight, full floor-length garment adopted by id⟨l⟩anders after the coming of the mis⟨s⟩ionaries. It is a copy of the "Mother Hubbard" that was worn by the ⟨m⟩issionary women. Sometimes it is ⟨m⟩ade with a yoke and set-in puffed ⟨sl⟩eeves. When it is made with a large ⟨pr⟩int it is often without the yoke, the ⟨n⟩eckline ranging from a boat neck ⟨to⟩ a Chinese collar, and the butterfly ⟨sl⟩eeve is lined with material of a ⟨so⟩lid color. To make muumuus with ⟨a⟩ yoke, use an old fashioned night-⟨gow⟩n pattern. The muumuu is a loose ⟨dre⟩ss and easy to make.

### THE LAVA LAVA

⟨N⟩ow if you would like to know ⟨wh⟩at the male in a Lava Lava looks ⟨like⟩ you should ask MISS ELLIE ⟨RU⟩SSO to show you a picture of her ⟨m⟩en with a Hawaiian in a lava lava. ⟨T⟩he more daring males may try a ⟨lava⟩ lava. This island dress for men ⟨cons⟩ists of a two-yard length of large ⟨flowe⟩r print cotton material. It is ⟨wrap⟩ped around the body, the top ⟨of⟩ the material being three inches ⟨abov⟩e the waist. The upper corner of ⟨the f⟩ree end of cloth is rolled into a ⟨tight⟩ knot and the cloth pulled tightly ⟨aroun⟩d the waist. To secure the gar-⟨ment,⟩ roll down the three-inch al-⟨lowan⟩ce from above the waist, enclos-⟨ing th⟩e knob. And believe it or not, ⟨the la⟩va lava stays in place. However, ⟨to en⟩sure peace of mind for those ⟨in ny⟩lon lava lavas for the first time ⟨a safe⟩ty pin may be strategically plac-⟨ed. I⟩ would put on my swim trunks

### THE HOLOKU

The holoku is a stately, more formal dress. The story is that the Hawaiian Queen who first adopted the muumuu was a woman of exceedingly large proportions. When she donned the "Mother Hubbard" she noticed with pride that he huge stomach hoisted the garment in front and lowered it behind. This affect delighted her and a fashion was born. The lowered back hem was purposely exaggerated until the dragging tail became a graceful full fledged train — a yard or two in length. Todays smartly styled holoku is characterized by its princess style lines and its long train, which has a wrist loop, to make graceful walking and dancing possible. The holoku may be made of any material, and the neck and sleeves of any style. Though it is a formal dress, it may be worn for any affair during the day or night. The holoku, because of its varied interpretations and neat graceful silhouette, is a most attractive garment for any woman of any age.

### THE HOLOMUU

The holomuu is a holoku without the long train. It is floor length and may easily be made with a princess styled housecoat pattern. This is perhaps the most practical form from the standpoint of wearability and utility of the styles.

### LUAU WEAR FOR MEN

Men may "go native" with brightly colored aloha shirts or may be dressed picturesquely as beachcombers. To emulate a beachcomber one may wear a tattered shirt and pants a colorful lei around the neck, and perhaps a bright blossom tucked behind one ear.

### OTHER ATTIRE

For women who want to go "South Pacific", sorongs and hula outfits are colorful attire.

**DON'T FORGET THE LUAU JUNE 19!!!**

Chapter 3

# THE 1970S

**PRESIDENTS**

| | |
|---|---|
| 1970 | W. Peter Lipscomb |
| 1971 | Lewis E. Brazelton |
| 1972 | Ben F. Chenault, Jr. |
| 1973 | Jay C. Grubb |
| 1974 | A. Fred Armstrong |
| 1975 | Glynn F. Martin |
| 1976 | A. T. Hubly, Jr. |
| 1977 | George G. Harris |
| 1978 | Herbert W. Varner |
| 1979 | Arnold E. Stremmel |

The 1970s were a time of great social upheaval in America. Youth movements marched against Corporate America and the Vietnam War. President Richard Nixon resigned. The floppy disc appeared, the first test-tube baby was born, and the original retail barcode was scanned. The Beatles broke up and *Saturday Night Fever* ignited a disco-dancing rage.

An Arab oil embargo sent oil prices soaring and stimulated an economic boom for Houston's energy industries. Demand for petrochemicals spawned a heyday "in the oilpatch." The city became legendary for its glitter and lavishness.

On September 20, 1973, Billie Jean King defeated Bobby Riggs (6-4, 6-3, 6-3) at the Houston Astrodome. It was called "the drop shot and volley heard around the world." A passion for tennis raged across the country, and also on the Briar Club courts.

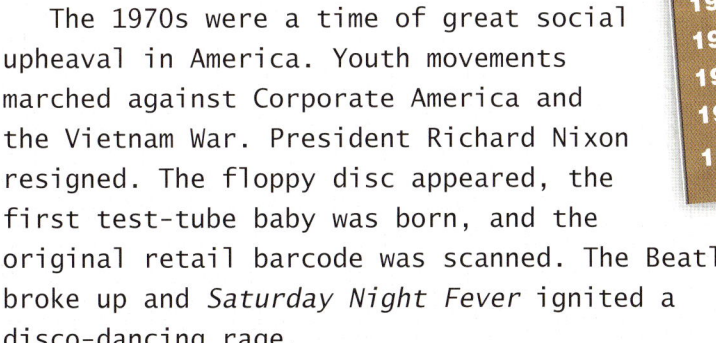

Tom Kamrath (tennis pro in the late seventies): There was a very colorful era there, with a lot of swearing, cussing, yelling, screaming, racket-breaking...the Billie Jean King versus Bobby Riggs match was a seminal moment in tennis. I saw that. The world thought it was a great media event. From a public relations standpoint, it was a bonanza for tennis.

I played pro a little bit and then began teaching. I taught at three different clubs in Texas before coming to The Briar Club. When I first came, The Briar Club was mainly a swimming and eating Club. Tennis was just getting started. In the late seventies, I came on full-time.

There were just four courts and no shop of any kind. There was just a breezeway between the pool and courts.

We filled in that area to make a pro shop. That was my first pro shop. We didn't have any teams. We did a little bit of inter-club play. There was no point system like you have now. Tennis was really just getting off the ground.

In the 1960s, tennis used to be divided. There was the amateur group and there was a small professional group that got paid to play. The USTA was trying to preserve the integrity of the game. There wasn't a lot of money to be made in playing professionally, so I turned to teaching. I found out I really loved teaching.

At The Briar Club, I had a client, Charlie Wilson. He was a good friend of my brother, Paul. Charlie was much older than us. He was determined to learn tennis and support me. He would come out for lessons as often as four times a week. He was a terrible tennis player but a wonderful guy. We would go have breakfast at the Avalon Drug Store and then work out on the courts for an hour.

Charlie was like my godfather. He was an independent oilman; lived on Wickersham. I'll never forget him.

**Nancy Guest:** Every Saturday morning, a dozen men showed up for the tennis round robin. You never had to look for a partner.

In this decade, a Past Presidents Committee was formed. It met three or four times a year for long-range planning and to make recommendations to the Board. The Club purchased a piano and a new sound system, resurfaced the tennis courts, completed the gazebo, and made gatehouse and kitchen modernizations. Members counted on the Friday Night Seafood Platter for $3.50.

In 1971, the Club drafted a new charter to accommodate the new state liquor laws, which allowed liquor to be sold by the glass.

**HAPPY HOURS FOR JANUARY**
**4 P.M. — 7 P.M.**
**DAILY, EXCEPT SUNDAY, MONDAY & THURSDAY**
**ONLY 60¢**

This is High Balls only (Scotch and Bourbon) Call drinks will be served at regular prices.

**NOTE:** Special Scotch and Bourbon is used only during the Happy Hour. However, it is as good or better than the liquor of other establishments. Make a habit of stopping off at the Briar Club when leaving the office for home.

Jay Grubb: The bar was small, but the lounge was too large, so sometimes you'd have to yell at the bartender for service. There were planter boxes where the south wall is now. There were hanging lights over them and nobody could resist giving them a push and watching them swing. It was open, and you'd really have to bellow to the bartender.

In the seventies, they chopped up the entire Briar Room with planter boxes, and they created little coves, but the waiters couldn't see anybody at any table. Couldn't get a food cart in there. Then, they wallpapered the entire east wall of the Briar Room. It had a tree pattern and they hung it upside down—yes, upside-down trees—and they tried to tell us that that was artistic, and we said no, trees don't grow upside-down. What a time. The Roaring Seventies.

John Neighbors: There was a snack bar with ceiling fans (where the sports bar is now). It was called the playdeck. It was one story and had a grille at one end, but the snack bar was grubby. There were always two garbage cans right out here where the grill is. It kept the atmosphere scented.

Jeff Cross: Our liquor license was suspended for three days because the inspectors couldn't find a jigger. We were free-pouring... Our bartender was using his coffee cup as a measure.

Bartenders are required to use a proper jigger so that the alcohol allowance is consistent. The Texas Alcoholic Beverage Commission wants to make sure your sales are commensurate with your purchases, because you have to pay tax on your sales.

The agents came by one day for a surprise inspection and said, "We'd like to see the jigger that you're using."

And hell, there wasn't one in the Club. Our bartender wanted to use a coffee cup.

◂ **BYOL Night at The Briar Club**
*Due to a technicality, The Briar Club found itself without a liquor license on Wednesday, October 6, 1971.*

*Completely undaunted, those members planning to dine that night produced fifths and miniatures to put some stimulation into the set-ups provided by the Club. Needless to say, quick action had everything back to normal by the next day.*

Peyton Burch: In the 1970s, the south wing of the Club was most of what we had. The Terrace Rooms were a kind of long room. The President's Room was the men's/women's locker room. The snack bar was fun—I worked in it—and the playdeck was the nicest place for teenagers, until someone realized you couldn't leave teenagers unsupervised.

## FOOD IN THE SNACK BAR

The Snack Bar will open in April on weekends only — 12 Noon until 6 P.M. The Snack Bar will be renovated, but will continue to serve Hamburgers, Hot Dogs, Sandwiches, Salads, Ice Cream and Beverages. Our recent questionnaire indicates by 90%, that our members enjoy our 75¢ Hamburger with Lettuce and Tomatoes and $1.00 for a Cheeseburger with Lettuce and Tomatoes. Our Hamburger meat is special ground, best quality 1/4 pound. On the whole our young men and ladies serving you are polite. A Snack Bar with many wet children is difficult and confusing. It is impossible to keep the floors dry, it is impossible to keep small children from dropping wrappers and litter on the floor. However, we try our best. The member can and should help.

* * * *
### PLAYDECK
If you are 16 years of age or older, you may use the Playdeck for playing cards. No smoking unless you are an adult. Self-service — self-policing. Please use recepticals. This area may be used for dining. However, children may use this room for dining only when accompanied by an adult.
* * * *

Playdeck

Snack Bar

They had a co-ed sauna and you could latch the door from inside or outside. The problem was keeping the teenagers out of it. There's a spa now. The problem is keeping the six-year-olds out of it.

Al Chivers: A lot of kids who came to The Briar Club also had memberships over at River Oaks. And oddly enough they'd come over here because it was more familial, more gregarious. This was where the sock hops took place. Back then, the Club was a really big place to bring a date. You could hear Ricky Nelson pouring out of the new speakers. There was a lot of music over the pool area and people really had a good time. The kids in the water were pushing and shoving—giving the lifeguards quite a time.

Our very popular and competent club manager, Al Chivers, C.C.M., is a member of the Club Managers Association of America and a former president of both the state and city C.M.A. groups. He is a charter member of the River Oaks Rotary Club. A Texan by birth, Mr. Chivers came to the Briar Club in 1957 after holding management positions in country clubs in San Antonio, Fort Worth and Tulsa.

Some families wanted to call the Kid's Club the Briar Patch, but that was the name of a gay Club on Greenbriar.

Jeannette Clift George: The Briar Club holds many memories for me. For years, the A.D. Players Theater Company has held dinners there. My husband, Lorraine George, loved lunches in the grille much more than the lunches I packed for him each morning (and found stacked out-of-date in the office refrigerator).

A special memory is of August 14, 1971. This was the day of our wedding. We had planned a small event. The wedding was held in River Oaks Baptist Church, and I had planned a small reception at The Briar Club, expecting twenty-five to thirty people. As the wedding guests arrived at the church, I asked a friend to call The Briar Club to say that the attendance might be more than expected... maybe thirty to forty people. In the end, there were 115 guests who lined the street and clamored around our wedding cake. And The Briar Club served everyone graciously. Weddings are miracles, and so are Briar Club receptions.

Lorraine George and Jeannette Clift George

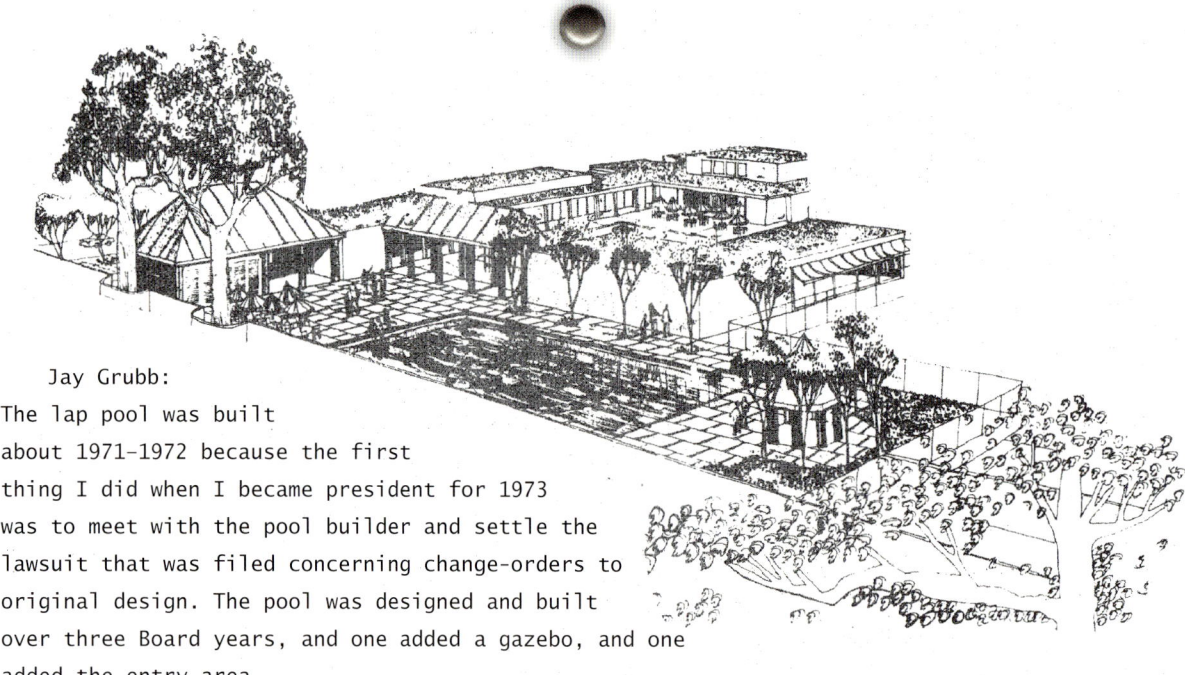

Jay Grubb:
The lap pool was built about 1971-1972 because the first thing I did when I became president for 1973 was to meet with the pool builder and settle the lawsuit that was filed concerning change-orders to original design. The pool was designed and built over three Board years, and one added a gazebo, and one added the entry area.

So the day after I became the Club president, Al Chivers called me and said, "The man from the pool company wants to meet with you about the money we allegedly owe."

And I said, "Good; tell him tomorrow at four o'clock and tell him we meet and we settle."

So Chivers said, "Well, what do you want me to do?"

And I said, "I want you to draw a cashier's check for half of that amount."

So when the fellow from the pool company came in, he had his attorney with him. I didn't know his attorney, but I knew his attorney's parents, which probably didn't hurt the discussion.

At the end of the day, the young man from the pool company said, "You guys owe me $14,000 for all the changes that have been added by various Boards."

He had on a leather jacket, dark glasses, fancy boots, and we sat back in the lounge and I said, "Would you care for a drink?"

He said, "No."

We visited a few minutes and finally I pulled out the check and laid it down and said, "You know I like to conclude matters of this nature."

"Oh," he said, "I couldn't do that. I'd like to visit with my attorney for a few minutes. Would you excuse us?"

I said, "No, Mr. Chivers and I will excuse ourselves, because we've got some things we need to look at around the Club, so we'll be back in a few minutes."

We did that, and when we came back, the pool company man said, "Does the offer for the drink still stand?"

I said, "Yes."

He said, "Good, because I've never had a seven-thousand-dollar martini."

And he signed the release and we handed him the seven-thousand-dollar check and that was the end of it.

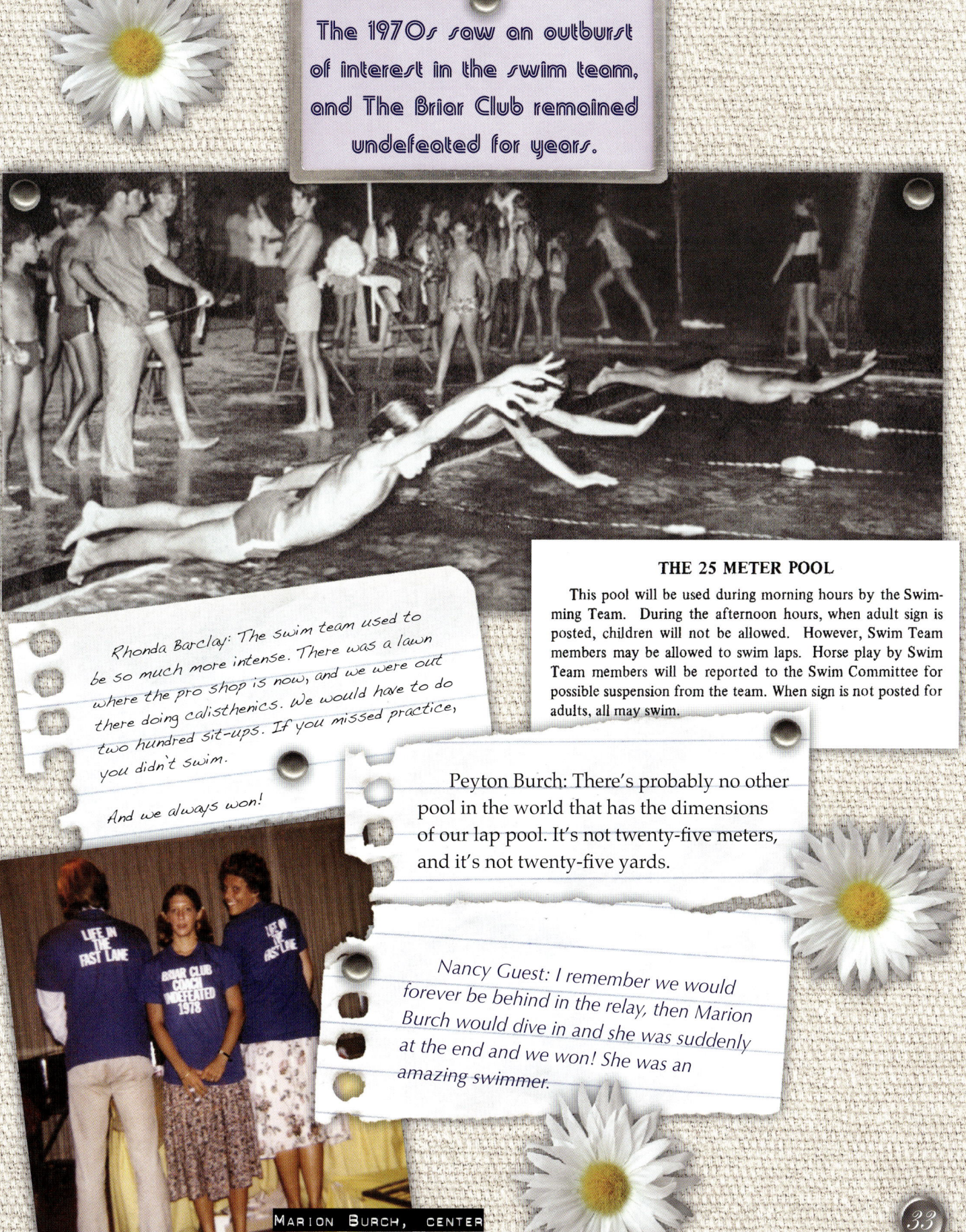

The 1970s saw an outburst of interest in the swim team, and The Briar Club remained undefeated for years.

**THE 25 METER POOL**

This pool will be used during morning hours by the Swimming Team. During the afternoon hours, when adult sign is posted, children will not be allowed. However, Swim Team members may be allowed to swim laps. Horse play by Swim Team members will be reported to the Swim Committee for possible suspension from the team. When sign is not posted for adults, all may swim.

Rhonda Barclay: The swim team used to be so much more intense. There was a lawn where the pro shop is now, and we were out there doing calisthenics. We would have to do two hundred sit-ups. If you missed practice, you didn't swim.

And we always won!

Peyton Burch: There's probably no other pool in the world that has the dimensions of our lap pool. It's not twenty-five meters, and it's not twenty-five yards.

Nancy Guest: I remember we would forever be behind in the relay, then Marion Burch would dive in and she was suddenly at the end and we won! She was an amazing swimmer.

MARION BURCH, CENTER

*Adrianne Atchley Kipp,
Judy Holke Atchley (now Nicklos),
and Daniel G. Atchley*

*Courtney Caswell*

Jeff Cross: We had three lifeguards per shift. I remember the day the chlorine gas tank sprung a leak. I was on my way to the airport to fly to Hawaii. I was leaving the house when the phone rang.

"The chlorine tank is leaking!"

I said, "Get the hell out of there!"

The fire department was over there in minutes. Fire trucks everywhere. That didn't happen too often, thank goodness.

One time Myron Steves' people burned up an electrical panel because they fired up a margarita machine they weren't supposed to have. But that didn't cause any great consternation. No fire trucks for that one. My heart always sinks when I drive by here and see fire trucks outside.

Barbara Caswell: Courtney Evans Caswell was an outstanding swimmer in the six-and-under. She swam here at The Briar Club until she was fourteen and never lost a race.

Most of our kids that were on the swim team came back and coached. The first year or two afterwards they'd be assistant coaches. They'd get a free lunch. The kids who went to college would come back and be head coaches.

*Walter Murtaugh and Marion Burch share the Briar Award.*

## SWIM TEAM BANQUET

On the evening of August 22nd the Briar Club honored its 1971 Paranha swim team. The affair was highlighted by a delicious buffet prepared by our Chef.

During the banquet the team and parents were entertained by an excellent film prepared and documented by Dr. J. M. Valenza. Presentation of the awards were made by the swimming committee: Dr. J. M. Valenza, Mr. & Mrs. Lawrence Athy and Mr. Jay C. Grubb.

Gary Festner gave a brief resume of the Briar Club team history whose record of 7 – 1 for this year is the best ever. Gary's overall average is 11 – 1, taking both the Dad's Club and the Briar Club Invitational. Coach Festner had nothing but praise for the team spirit and their exceptional effort.

The John Buckley award was won by James Doyle and Susan McClure. Sportsmanship: Billy White and Susie Wright.

The Al Chivers All Briar Award: Walter Murtaugh & Marion Burch.

Outstanding Swimmer: Bobby Wood & Karen Krimm.

Captain: Nancy Pierson.

Co-Captain: Michelle Bambace.

**Marion Burch:** Swim team was absolutely the most fun thing to do. There was amazing camaraderie. We used to pile into the cars for trips to the meets, and when I was little I got to sit on the console of Nancy Pierson's car. We'd sing the whole way there. Win the meet. Sing the whole way home.

I used to say to my parents, "I need to be dropped off at the Briar Club at 7 a.m. and don't you dare pick me up before 7 p.m."

*Marion Burch, left*

**Randy Burch:** The last year Marion coached she told me she was very concerned because they had not lost a meet in five years, and she worried that she had not taught them how to lose. She thought that was an injustice.

*Peyton Burch: My sister, Marion Burch, was the Briar Club swim coach from the time she was fourteen (about 1976) until she was twenty-two. She was eight years old when we joined The Briar Club, and she'd been swimming AAU since she was four. Marion used to go to school in a bathing suit.*

*She and Mike Caswell rejuvenated the whole Club swim league. I used to bet people all the time that my sister's swim team was going to trounce theirs. The kids that swam for Marion knew how to dive, how to turn, how to stroke. They knew how to take the seconds off. I always won my bets.*

← *Marion Burch in the lifeguard stand*

*Peyton Burch: My father was here every time Marion swam or coached. He was on the sidelines every single time. For that they give out the Randolph Burch Award for Best Swimmer each year.*

Barbara Beich: Do you remember the high dive? It was scary-high. And Mike Caswell was Mr. Splash. He'd go up and do a cannonball. Water the plants.

*High dive, Elizabeth Edmiston and Marty Hricik*

## Swim Team

36

*Lucky divers—$5.00 winners are Tom Grubb, Billy White, and Scott Thompson*

# Derby Day

**WHISPERS**

BRIAR CLUB

PUBLISHED MONTHLY — MAY, 1977

**RESERVATIONS CLOSED**

Derby Day at the Briar Club is more fun than being at Louisville. SATURDAY, MAY 7, 1977. A southern buffet will be served from 12:30 until 2:30. (please do not plan to arrive before 12:00 Noon). Music by Charlie Prause—Mint Juleps. Your first Mint Julep is included in the party price. $8.00 per person plus gratuity and tax. SOLD OUT—STANDING ROOM ONLY. SORRY, NO CANCELLATIONS!!

COLOR TELEVISIONS · TIP SHEETS · DAILY DOUBLE · PARI MUTUAL

Briar Club odds will be posted every 30 minutes.

Jay Grubb: Derby Day was very popular in the seventies and early eighties. You couldn't get in here with a stick. There were several televisions carrying the race. They had the Club odds, which were different than the track odds. You had to have somebody upstairs to see what they were doing, somebody with enough math to work through the Club odds. This was most often Ben Chenault. They published a betting sheet, and it was headed "Big Al Shakes and Chivers."

Bingo and Derby Day were huge. And now we don't do that at all. Times change. The Bingo thing is not like it was. They used to play every Thursday night. Rotary sponsored it. There was a state law that Bingo has to be licensed to regulate it, and it has to be sponsored by a nonprofit organization, so we had the River Oaks Rotary Club to be the sponsor. Thursday night was the big night around here. The buffet was $4.95 and the Bingo prizes went into the several hundreds of dollars.

DERBY DAY

Fred Carpenter: *You didn't fool with Bingo.*

Tom Gillette: We paid fifty dollars a month to Rotary to sponsor Bingo nights. The turnout for Bingo was huge, and the prizes were even bigger. Those prizes were paid for by the Club.

I said that the Bingo cards should be self-sustaining. We shouldn't be using membership dues to pay for Bingo prizes. The prizes should be determined by the intake. So we set a higher price, a quarter or fifty cents, for the cards, and you should have heard the uproar!

MR. JOHN DEASON SHOWS HIS FIFTY-SIX-NUMBER BLACKOUT TO WIN $500.

Tom Gillette: It was a Thursday night get-together. The menu was way under-priced and fairly elaborate.

39

Peyton Burch: Mel Burns was the best bartender this Club ever had—hands down. Everybody turned up on Friday afternoons for Happy Hour in the old dark, dark bar because of Mel. He had personality. You didn't know what he'd say to you, but his drinks were always good. And he knew when to turn it off and turn it on. He'd sling remarks with all the men, but when a woman walked into the room he was charming and gracious as he could be.

My grandmother used to come here every day at five o'clock to have her one drink for medicinal purposes. Everybody said Mel made the best drinks they'd ever had. He knew how to mix drinks. He knew which bottle of bourbon had which taste and which effect.

He was my first boss. A bunch of us boys worked for Mel. We did everything. My first job here was cutting the lawn and cleaning the locker rooms and emptying the garbage cans. I was fifteen years old and worked every day from ten to three, and at three-fifteen, I was in the swimming pool. We had a blast! We were fifteen years old, making more money than we had a right to, working five or six hours a day. I vacuumed every inch of this Briar Club.

There were a lot of times Mel Burns had reason to fire the lot of us boys, and he never did. He was boss, friend, and mentor. Finally, he had to move away from bartending because the damn bar was so dark and his eyesight was going. I will not tell you what he called me! It was a very endearing term to him and me, but it wasn't something I'd ever say aloud again, *ever*.

---

**Mel's Famous Bloody Mary**

8 oz. Pure Lemon Juice
5 oz. Lea & Perrins
2 tbsp. Accent
1/2 tsp. Salt
1 tsp. Celery Salt
2 qts. Tomato Juice
1 10-oz. can Beef Bouillon Soup

Fill the rest with vodka, shake well, and chill. Makes one gallon. Keeps refrigerated about two weeks.

---

**GALIANO ACCEPTS MEL BURNS COCKTAIL**

Mel Burns, our bartender, put his many talents to work and came up with a delicious new cocktail, the Zsa Zsa. The Galiano Company is going to use Mel's recipe in their next publication. Those of you who haven't tried the Zsa Zsa will be in for a most pleasant surprise.

---

Jay Grubb: When Mel's bar moved to the current bar/lounge area, we named the room the Renaissance Room. It was eventually called the Golden Room because no one could spell "Renaissance."

**Jay Grubb:** Walter singing "Happy Birthday" was a "delight" not to be missed. He had a voice worse than a cow!

**Tom Gillette:** One time we hired a maître d'. He was a black man, Walter, and always liked flashy vests. He had been the maître d' at Chez Orleans, which used to be one of the better restaurants down on Westheimer, right before you got to the railroad tracks. One night my wife and I were in the Terrace Room and I asked him to turn the lights down because it was very bright, and that just wasn't consistent with casual dining in the evening.

He replied, "Oh no sir, I cannot do that. If we turn the lights down, then I can't see the flies when they drop in the soup!"

I said, "Say that again?" And he did! And I said, "Turn the damn lights down!"

## Happy Hour

period of adjustment,
wind-down-time,
or what ever you want to call it,
at the Briar Club it's
5 - 7 PM
Tuesday through Friday.
Enjoy ½ price drinks,
complimentary hors d'oeuvres,
chips 'n dips. Salud!

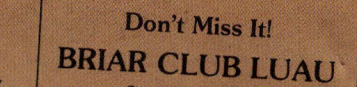

---

*Briar Dance Club*
*Summer Dance — Formal*

SATURDAY, MAY 26th
RUSSELL JACKSON — ORCHESTRA
COCKTAILS 8:30 — DANCING 9 TILL 1 A.M.
MIDNIGHT BREAKFAST AT 11:30
BAR DRINKS
GRATUITY AND SALES TAX
ALL FOR ONLY
$30.00 PER COUPLE
MAKE YOUR RESERVATIONS NOW
Come and Join In The Fun
Jacque Johnson — 462-3820

**NOTICE**
FOR LIMITED TIME ONLY —
BRIAR CLUB MEMBERSHIPS ARE AVAILABLE
SOCIAL (Non-Equity) $400.00 Initiation Fee
PLUS Monthly Dues - $45.00
Membership — ALL CLUB HOUSE ACTIVITIES TO INCLUDE SWIMMING
RESIDENT (Equity) $1,000.00 Initiation Fee
PLUS Monthly Dues - $37.50
Membership — FULL PRIVILEGES, INCLUDING TENNIS AND SWIMMING
All Membership subject to $20.00 monthly minimum (Food & Bar C...)
Remember all memberships are limited — Get a Friend to Join

---

**Don't Miss It!**
**BRIAR CLUB LUAU**
Saturday, June 9th
**Ono Ono Luau Kaukau Nani**
A feast to celebrate a joyous occasion where good Fellowship reigns supreme
Bring your Wahine for...
HAWAIIAN...
"On the...
at the B...
$9.00 PER...
Includes Mai...
Pu Pu Pl...
(Hawaiian style...
An Exotic Poly...
Pineapple...
Baked Fish with...
Kalua Pig — whole, ro...
Chicken H...
Malinini Pai (Cream...
Pineapple Sticks with...
Spring S...
Lomi Sal...
Sweet Potatoes
Laulaus (Tora lea...
Kono — c...
Plus Other D...
MAIN CLUBHOUS...
DANCING TO — FRED...
THE HAWAIIAN ECHO...
LUAU DAN...
Music and hors d'oeuvres
Dress: Aloha Shirts, Muu...
Reservations Essenti...
SORRY, NO CANC...

---

**Jay Grubb:** In the early 1970s, the property to our South, where the Park St. John condos are now, came on the market. There was a uniform supply company. They rented and leased uniforms for various industries. Well, there was a period of time when they decided to move their plant elsewhere and all that property became available.

Nancy Cunningham's husband owned that property and had that business there. The Briar Club could have picked it up for five dollars per square foot and they didn't. They didn't have the money. It was that simple. It was a lot of money back then.

Well, and we had a Board that wouldn't buy six light bulbs at a time, so they weren't about to buy that.

---

**Jay Grubb:** The first time somebody wanted fitness I was on the Board. So the Club sent out a questionnaire (thinking about bicycles to ride) and asked if there was any interest. They got 105 affirmative responses. So the next communication that went out solicited a check for one hundred dollars per person, to get the project up and running. My memory is the Club received three checks.

## Chapter 4

### WHISPERS
**BRIAR CLUB**
APRIL 1981

**CHILDREN'S Easter Egg Hunt**
8 years old and under.
Sunday, April 12
Lots of beautiful eggs and favors!!!
DON'T BE LATE
1:30 PM
REFRESHMENTS
For Members' Children and Grandchildren
GUESTS ARE WELCOME
RESERVATIONS ONLY
622-3667

---

**Pool Side Only**
TWO DRINKS FOR THE PRICE OF ONE
Friday, June 6 (2 p.m. til 5 p.m.)
Signed _____ (only with this coupon)

**Pool Side Only**
TWO DRINKS FOR THE PRICE OF ONE
Friday, June 20 (2 p.m. til 5 p.m.)
Signed _____ (only with this coupon)

**Pool Side Only**
TWO DRINKS FOR THE PRICE OF ONE
Friday, June 13 (2 p.m. til 5 p.m.)
Signed _____ (only with this coupon)

**Pool Side Only**
TWO DRINKS FOR THE PRICE OF ONE
Friday, June 27 (2 p.m. til 5 p.m.)
Signed _____ (only with this coupon)

---

**The Briar Ladies Organization presents**
**Citizens against Crime**
*Ideas for Self-Protection*
Wednesday, June 8, 1988
Hospitality Hour - 10:30 to 11:30 A.M.
Followed by Program, Lunch & Briar
$8.50 inclusive

Please call your reservation in early.
622-3667
One day notice on cancellations

---

**Be Our Annual Valentine**

and come to our First Annual Valentine's Day Party if you were a New Member in 1981. Old members come on out and welcome the new! Sunday, February 14th 6-9 PM / Dancing, Cocktails and substantial hors d'oeuvres. $5.00++/person. A good time to be had by all!

---

**The Briar Ladies Organization presents "Show and Tell"**
View the special talents of our own Briar Club ladies... paintings of all kinds, needlecraft, etc... some for sale!
Wednesday, November 12, 1986
Hospitality 10:30-11:30 A.M. Program & Luncheon from 11:30 — then BRIAR!
$8.50 inclusive
Menu
Spinach Salad
Puffed pastry Shell filled with Seafood

---

**LET'S TALK TURKEY!**

**CLUB BORROWING** - If you have anything borrowed from the Club, please return as soon as possible. Items out are Santa and Easter Bunny outfits, and a coffin.

---

**New Orleans Jazz Brunch**
Sunday, November 10, 1985
11:30 a.m. — 1:30 p.m.
$14.95++ per person
(inclusive)
Guests Welcome
Live Jazz Band

Champagne Peach Bowle
Brandy Milk Punch
Eggs Benedict
Spanish Eggs
Seafood Quiche
Sausage - Bacon
Broccoli Souffle
Fresh Fruit Tray
French Bread
Sweetrolls
Pralines, Eclaires and Petit Fours

R.S.V.P. 622-3667
Cancellation Deadline is 24 hours in advance of theme party
Committee:
Maria & Richard D'Antoni
Mary & Larry Peterson
Dolby and B.J. Willingham

---

**CHILDREN'S CHRISTMAS PARTY**
Sunday, December 4
11:30 A.M. - 2:00 P.M.
Patio Room
Santa Claus
Christmas Stocking Decorating
Balloon Art
Sandwiches, Cookies and Punch
A Fun, Festive Time for Everyone!
$2.50++ per person
R.S.V.P. 622-3667
24 hour cancellation required

Santa's Helpers:
Julie & Steven Harris, Chairmen
Janet & Dave Amend, Peg & Robert Bennett
Cinda & Grant Buce, Lee & Jot Couch
Julie & Tracy Coffey, Mary & Greg Hobbs
tty & Richard Hemingway, Carol & Sterling Minor
Ann & Tom Servos

**MEMBERS' CHRISTMAS PARTY**
Sunday, December 18
6:00 P.M. - 10:00 P.M.
Briar Room
Cocktails
Heavy Hors d'Oeuvres
Christmas Carols
Music for dancing
A Glittering Night for A
$10.00++ per couple
$20.00++ per guest
Includes food, wine, bar drink and a wonderful time.
R.S.V.P. 622-3667
24 hour cancellation require

---

**CAJUN SHRIMP PEEL**
Friday, September 23, 1988
7:00 P.M. - 11:00 P.M.
$17.95++ Per Person
PATIO ROOM & POOLSIDE
RESERVATIONS PLEASE
622-3667
24 hour cancellation required

# The 1980s

Ronald Reagan presided over two terms as president during the 1980s. He handed the baton to Houston's own George Bush, Sr. in January 1989. Video games, minivans, and tanning salons took root in this decade. A "shop 'til you drop" culture created economic frenzy, Madonna hit the stage, and AIDS emerged as a terrifying epidemic.

The census of 1980 registered over one and a half million residents in Houston. Cathy Whitmire was the first woman to become mayor and she hired Lee Brown away from Atlanta to trounce crime in the city.

The Briar Club witnessed its own genteel revolution during these years. Those members who enjoyed dining and Bingo were sometimes at odds with those members who prioritized the swimming, tennis, and outdoor activities. There were disagreements regarding where Club funds should be spent. These growing pains compelled changes, which led to a better family Club for all.

There were major renovations to the existing campus as well. The swimming pools were improved and the lap pool heated, and the high dive was removed for safety. Three new Omni tennis courts were completed as Phase I of the long-range planning proposals. A new computer system was installed.

### PRESIDENTS

| Year | President |
|------|-----------|
| 1980 | William W. Caldwell |
| 1981 | George A. Donaldson |
| 1982 | Fred F. Morgan, Jr. |
| 1983 | Fred A. Carpenter, Jr. |
| 1984 | Thomas W. Gillette |
| 1985 | J. Stanley Taylor |
| 1986 | C. Wayne Bardwell |
| 1987 | Jeff J. Cross II |
| 1988 | Dorothy M. Porter |
| 1989 | Lee E. Hancock |

**WELCOME NEW MEMBERS**

**Skyboxes, Briar Club Style** for **Monday Night Football.** Call 622-3667 to sign up, or just show up in the Bar. Free hors d'oeuvres, and the game will be right there, on our nearly *life-size* screen.

**The Briar Club 1987 Summer Programs**
- Summer Fun Camp
- Junior Tennis Program
- Swim Team
- Swimming Lessons

**Briar Dance Club**
welcomes Briar Club Members to attend the December Dance on Saturday, Dec. 3.
*8:00 - 12:00 PM*
Breakfast 11:00 PM
$50.00 Per Couple
R.S.V.P. Mimmie Higginbotham
723-8194

Virginia Berry

Marjorie Cross

**EVERY THURSDAY — IS FAMILY NIGHT**

Buffet Dinner—Only $7.00* with Reservations—
$8.50* Without Reservations— Call 622-3667

Dinner Served from 6:00 p.m. until 8:00 p.m.
Reservations *must* be in before 5:00 p.m.

*New Price

PLAY BRIAR WIN CASH, PLUS LUNCHEONS AND DINNERS. NO CASH POT UNDER $25.00

Reservations Please!!
June 5th, 12th, 19th and 26th

---

**FANTASY ROOM**
Available by Reservations ONLY

Whatever your needs are — Inquire about this room.
Bridge Groups of 3 tables or more*
Seminars - Cocktail Receptions
Luncheon - Dinners
Call to reserve Now — Ask Jacki for details.
The FANTASY ROOM has been named this due to the ORIGINAL wall prints named — Hungarian Fantasy!

---

January 27th - **Wienerisch Delights,** from the land of Tirol, Austria, comes...

**Kopfsalat mit Essig Und Öl**
*Boston Lettuce with Oil & Vinegar*

**Wiener Schnitzel**
*Milk Fed Veal, Breaded & Sauteed in Butter*

**Röst Kartoffeln**
*Pan Roasted Potatoes*

**Grüne Bohnen mit Speck**
*Fresh Green Beans Sauteed with Bacon and Fine Herbs*

**Apfel Strudel mit Vanilla Sauce**

13.75

---

— SUNDAY —
BUFFET DINNER featuring
Prime Rib of Beef, Au Jus
11:45 UNTIL 2:30 P.M. — Reservations 622-3667

EVERY FRIDAY
SEAFOOD BUFFET
THAT WILL DELIGHT YOU AND YOUR GUESTS
Reservations 622-

If you try them you will Agree!
**STEAK NIGHT**
Most Popular Night of the Week

BY SPECIAL DEMAND
EVERY SATURDAY —
Spaghetti With all Kinds of Sauce Served With a Glass of Wine
$5.75* — Children $3.50
We Fix — You Match Served With Garlic Bread, Green Salad Served in the Patio Room
6:00 p.m.
RESERVATIONS 622-3667
ONLY $5.75* plus Tax and Gratuity
Dress Casual
This is a promise of a fun-filled evening
— Invite your friends.
ALSO — FRIDAY NIGHT SPECIAL
Check When Making Your Reservations —

SPAGHETTI NIGHT

EVERY WEDNESDAY
PLANTATION BUFFET DINNER
(Informal Dining in Patio Room)

**Family Fun Night...**
EVERY THURSDAY EXCEPT THURSDAY, DEC. 25
Buffet ...... 6:00 P.M.
Games ...... 8:00 P.M.
Buffet Dinner — Only $7.00 with Reservations —
Call 622-3667

EVERY SATURDAY IN DECEMBER
**Happy Hour**
$1.25 Drink          2:00 PM til 7:00 PM
HOUSE BRANDS — NO CALL

---

**Wildgame Dinner February 5, 1985**

Clean out your freezers before Hunting season. Donate your wild game to the Club for our Annual Wildgame Dinner. We depend on your donations.

HUNTERS - what a better reason to endure the hardships of hunting than to supply badly needed food for the Wildgame Dinner!!

Make your reservations now!

---

**The Briar Club's Wild(est) Game Dinner**
February 4, 1986 at 7:00 p.m.
R.S.V.P. 622-3667

Game Wardens:
Cletus Dodd
Fred Duncan
Bill Evans
Lee Hancock
Rick Leachman
Dan Parker
Larry Peterson
Steve Rice

All Hunters, Would Be Hunters & Guests welcome for an evening of feasting, gaming and entertaining

$23.00++ per person - open Bar
WILD GAME DONATIONS ACCEPTED

44

**THE BRIAR CLUB**
July, 1989

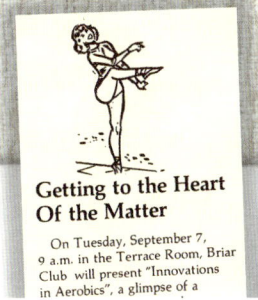

**Getting to the Heart Of the Matter**

On Tuesday, September 7, 9 a.m. in the Terrace Room, Briar Club will present "Innovations in Aerobics", a glimpse of a

**Grand Opening**
**The Briar Club Fitness Center**
**Saturday, July 1, 1989**
Free Aerobics classes for the day with instruction on weight machines and work-out programs.

- 9:30 A.M. — Super Work-out (Featuring Lynn Hargrove)
- 10:00 A.M. — Water Aerobics
- 12:45 P.M. — Low Impact (Featuring Tina Kelinske)
- 5:00 P.M. — Free Consultations Sign-ups, Etc.

ome by and check out our beautiful new facilities. na Kelinske, our Fitness Director, will be there to show you around, answer your questions, and listen to your comments and suggestions.

*Bill Evans, Cletus Dodd (tall one), Dan Clements (general manager), Page Piland, John Manry, Lee Hancock, Ginny Cranford, Joe Santamaria, Dorothy Porter, Jim Hodges, Randy Burch, and Fritz Beich.*

**FITNESS CENTER INFORMATION**

As everyone is aware, the Club is expanding — to up-grade its present facilities and provide new ones. One of the new facilities will be a large Fitness and Aerobics Room. We will begin to form aerobics classes now. Tina Kelinske will be the new Fitness Director. Tina is a recent graduate of Southwest Texas State University, with a Bachelor of Science Degree in Recreational Administration. She has over 2½ years of experience in teaching aerobics and is certified by the Aerobics and Fitness Association of America.

All interested members are asked to drop off their comments and suggestions to Tina, at the front office, as to what you would like to see offered when we open our new facility in the middle of June.

Plans and financing for the most ambitious building program ever undertaken by the Club were approved. The new kitchen was installed. An informal dining area, a new snack bar, a two-story Fitness Center with locker and exercise rooms, and the President's Room were added. The Patio Room was repainted and refurbished, and new artwork decorated the Club walls. The Briar Ladies contributed a bounty of serving pieces—slotted spoons, carving knives, heavy silver chafing dishes—for the infamous Sunday Brunch.

In 1981, the Club hired a new executive chef, Alfred Wolfgang Atschreiter, who trained in Austria. He launched a series of Wild Game Dinners. Members were invited to clean out their freezers, and the hodge-podge contents could be brought to the Club for preparation. Wild Game Dinners became a popular annual event at The Briar Club and continued on into the mid-nineties.

Tom Gillette: As president, I pushed to purchase the property on the corner of Saint Street. It came on the market and we paid a dear price: six hundred thousand dollars, or thirty-five dollars per square foot. Compare that with five dollars per square foot ten years earlier.

It's top dollar, but if we could get both corners, then sooner or later, we'd have the properties in between. The one was an automobile show room owned by a fellow named Monty Frost. His lot came on the market fifteen years later. The veterinary clinic came on the market seventeen years later. Those properties were worth more to us than anyone else.

If anyone asked what I did for The Briar Club, that was the thing—buying that corner.

I want to give credit to some of the older members, long deceased, that really kept the Club going during that period—specifically, Bill Caldwell and Arnold Stremmel.

It was Arnold Stremmel who personally loaned the Club fifteen thousand dollars when things were lean so that the Club didn't have to go on COD to meet payroll. The good thing is, he was repaid.

*Myron and Mary Louise Steves*

## From Venetian To Briar

All December party guests please note our new Briar Room, (formerly The Venetian Room).

Remodeling budget considerations have resulted in this happy outcome. The renovated parquet area makes for great dancing—and the carpet remains to soften noises in the remaining area for dining and conversation.

—Physical Properties Committee

# Happy Anniversary

*The Briar Club*

### Briar Club Poorhouse Party

**Come commiserate with your fellow taxpayers!**

April 15, 1986
5:30 PM – 8:30 PM
33¢ Drinks!
Hors d'ouvres

---

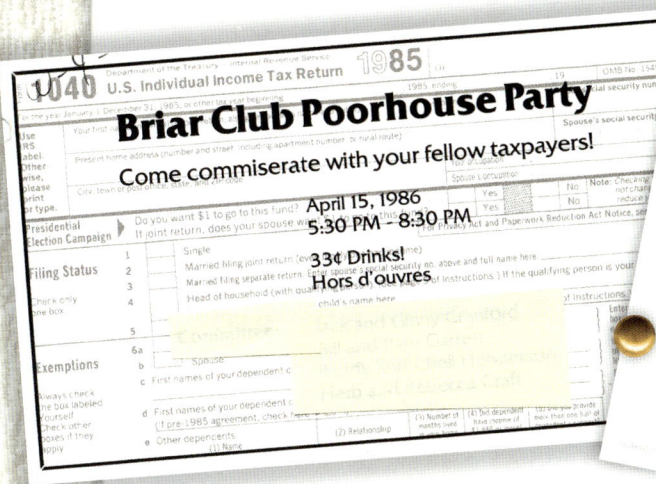

Myron Steves: My company was called Surplus Lines. The substandard liability that no one wants to insure—we did that. We wrote this insurance on a wholesale basis.

One year we had our Christmas party here at The Briar Club. I enjoyed a play on words. For our invitations, I turned Surplus Lines into Surplus *Lion*. Then I called one of these circus people and had him bring by a big sedated lion. We had him back there in the Briar Room. A lion. Right in the middle of the floor.

The circus fellow brought a chimp too, by the way. I kind of liked that chimp. He was smart and he had a taste for beer. I think they kept the Surplus Lion in business by renting the chimp, too. The chimp got a little unruly and climbed up on me and kissed me! A little while after I went into the restroom and there was the chimp. He went by himself, and jumped up on the sink waiting for someone to turn on the water so he could wash his hands.

*Myron Steves and a chimp*

---

**HAPPY HOUR LOUNGE ONLY**

Happy Hour 2 p.m. till 6 p.m.
Every week day
except Monday.

Hiballs . . . . . . . . . . . . . $1.00
Beer . . . . . . . . . . . . . . . . .75
Call Drinks at regular price.
Anytime Margarita . . . $2.25

---

Jay Grubb: On April 15th every year, we had a four-o'clock deal for dollar drinks—all drinks for one dollar. All the waiters went around with their pockets out. There was a hearse in the circle drive with a casket hanging out. We were all celebrating tax day. There were hundreds of people here!

Jay Grubb: After Mr. Chivers, the manager of the Club for several years came Hans Kohler, who was, I assure you, very German. Hans was very good, very direct, and I enjoyed listening to him. He would say, "I terminated so-and-so today, Mr. G."

And I said, "You did?"

And he said, "Yes! And he left in a big *huffy*!"

*Club brochure, 1985. Manager Hans Kohler, far right.*

Tom Gillette: Hans Kohler once came to me and said, "We have to get a new chef—ours just gave us two weeks' notice." The next morning, Hans approached me again and said, "Our chef is leaving in three days." Next day, Hans came into the office and said, "The chef just left on the bus this morning."

I said, "Hans, what is the story?"

And Hans said, "His girlfriend's husband just got out of Huntsville."

Nancy Guest: I liked that Hans Kohler. So efficient! He walked around and he knew everything that was going on. He could have run the whole German army.

## THE BRIAR CLUB OKTOBERFEST

...erful evening at the Club on October 21. The food was German and out of this world. The band was the Henry Tannenberger Orchestra and was terrific. Everyone feels that this should be an annual affair at the Club.

### TENNIS

The men's tennis team is now leading the Memo... League after beating its old rival, Memorial Forest,... margin.

| STANDINGS | WON | LOST |
|---|---|---|
| Briar Club | 26 | 4 |
| Nottingham | 25 | 5 |
| Wilchester | 24 | 6 |
| Memorial Forest | 26 | 6 |
| Net Set | 10 | 10 |
| Memorial Drive | 7 | 23 |
| Memorial Bend | 7 | 23 |
| Memorial West | 6 | 19 |
| Memorial Townhouses | 4 | 16 |
| Lakeside C.C. | 2 | 18 |

The men's "B" team has now won 13 and l...
The women's team is tied for 2nd in their...
3 record, 3½ games behind Wilchester

Luncheon will be serve...
Christmas Eve at the Cl...
Close at 3 p.m.
The Club will be closed December 25...

### DECEMBER FOOD SPECIALS

TUESDAY EVENINGS
... Strip Sirloin ............... $4.95
...INGS
........................ $2.75
........................ $3.75
........................ $3.50
........................ $4.95

PRICE OF ONE
...cial)
...TURDAY, DECEMBER 30

HOURS
...7 p.m.
...onday, Thursday
— 60¢
bar liquor only

48

Nancy Guest: We used to come here every Friday just for the gumbo.

Once we had an Asian chef and he used to tease the kids. On the menu there was spaghetti with marinara sauce. And he would ask the kids, "Can I get you rattlesnakes with marijuana sauce?"

Barbara Beich: There was a party every few months to welcome new members. I met some of my favorite friends there. It was at night, and that was for adults.

Then on opening day for the pool each spring, they'd have a huge party for the whole family. They had hot dogs and games. They'd throw money in the pool. The kids loved that. Then they'd throw beers in the pool. The adults loved that. They were drowning each other to wrestle the cans from one another. Then they threw fish into the pool and gave the kids plastic bags to collect them, but the fish went belly-up too fast. Goldfish. They floated to the top before the kids could get them into their bags. I told you we had a little chlorine problem.

After we scooped out the dead fish, they put up a sheet and made a sort of fashion runway. This was the Best Legs contest for the men. All the husbands would walk through with their legs swinging. People were cheering and clapping, and I suppose the winner was selected by the clap-o-meter. Fritz won the trophy one year: 1983.

Other Summer Activities:
Movies
Jam Sessions
Cook-Outs
Shrimp Peels, etc.

**Early Bird Swimmers and Tennis Players**

New Times. The tennis courts and 25-meter pool will open at 7:00 AM on a daily basis (Tues.-Sun.) for "Early Birds". "Early Bird" Coffee Service on Weekends: Free coffee on the Playdeck on Saturdays and Sundays from 7:00 AM to 11:00 AM.

**WELCOME NEW MEMBERS**

# Splash Day!

*"Ready or not, here I come!"*—Kolby Beich

## Splash Into Spring!

On Splash Day, May 2, come and help open the Family Pool. Floaty Races! Nutty Buddy Races! (you won't believe this one) Grossly Greased Watermelon Races! Barbeque Buffet! And get the scoop on Scuba at our poolside demonstration, while you down a Daiquiri (summer's first) from Gil's Daiquiri Dasher. Reservations 622-3667. Deadline for cancellations is Saturday, May 1, at 5:00 PM. Adults 8.95++; Children 6-11 4.95++; under, no charge

Marion Burch: On Splash Day, we had races in the pool. You'd have to swim down to the other end, chew a cracker, whistle, then swim back. Or sometimes you had to push an apple ahead of you with your chin. First the kids did it, then the adults raced, too. After that, someone threw a greased watermelon into the deep end of the pool and forty kids dove in to retrieve it. Some of the mothers did a synchronized swimming performance. It was non-stop fun.

Those were the days with no big lists of rules and regulations, and everything worked out fine. The Briar Club was start-to-finish a safe and positive environment.

LET'S GO "BRIAR CUDAS"!

Susan Hancock: *On Splash Day, we used to do a show for everybody. One year we were the Aquettes! We were a synchronized swimming splendor. Eight of us girls drove into the Club through the back gate—which didn't exist then—no gate then. We came in on an MGTD convertible! Who was there? Meg Rice (my twin sister), Susan Hancock (me), Marsha Parker, Terrell Hill, Joann Flynn, Jan Parker maybe... I can't remember. There were tons of people here.*

*We all had swim caps on and matching swimsuits and robes, and we got off the MG and slipped into a line at the edge of the pool. Then we dropped our robes and swish!, dove one after another into the water. We paddled into the shallow water for our routine. And all we did was walk! But everyone watched our arms, waving this way and that, like we were Esther Williams reincarnated. The Aquettes were big-time. We were fabulous. Not even fair to the young men.*

*The men were so jealous they joined us the next year. We called them the Aqua-nuts.*

Above: John Eyberg

Left: Jim and Will Nolen

Barbara Beich: They used to put a band on top of the baby pool. They put a bridge over the pool, for parties. They were fun parties! See if you can find any pictures of the Toga Party. It was a scream. People brought their togas that they'd had in college, and they were a little tight…

TOGA! TOGA! TOGA!

## First in the Water

The Briar Club Swim Team had another fantastic season this year, finishing with a *perfect 6-0 Record!!* Undefeated for the third year—League Champions for the 5th straight year, The Briar Club is already looking to next season's challenge.

*Barbara Caswell:* Before we did the swim team, Phillip Dreesen did it, for years. He had three daughters, all fabulous swimmers. And he's a fabulous pediatrician here in Houston. In those days, swim team was an enormous commitment. It used to last ten weeks.

I remember one year there was a new team around—Briargrove, I think it was—and they wanted to get into the Club league. So we said, "Ok, we'll swim y'all." It was the beginning of the season and our kids were in great shape.

So these kids all walked into the Club with leg weights on—we knew we were history. We lost. That was the first time we lost since we were members.

*JoJo Dreesen*

## SWIM TEAM NEWS

The Briar Club Swim Team is undefeated again! Head Coach Julie Arbuthnot and her assistants Beth Cole, David Houston, Jody Johnston and Matthew Newtown are excited about retaining the Country Club Championship trophy for the 8th year in a row.

The Briar Club is represented by 160 children (99 under the age of 8). There will be a banquet July 1st, and all swimmers will be rewarded for their participation and achievement.

**CONGRATULATIONS TO BRIAR CLUB SWIM TEAM**

FIRST IN COUNTRY CLUB DIVISION

*Mike Caswell:* I raised four kids in that pool, and I ruined three or four thousand dollars' worth of cowboy boots pulling wet kids *out* of that pool.

Barbara and I were chairs of the Swim Committee for years. So I pushed and pushed for updating the system out there.

We didn't have the chemicals under control. You either had a green pool or kids with green hair. If the pool got too green, we'd pull out the kids and shock it.

We'd have to physically throw in blocks of chlorine. Every year we used to give out a trophy for greenest hair.

I finally convinced them to dig out that pool. They had a one-and-a-half-inch drain for that whole pool. Like trying to suck a basketball through a garden hose. We put in a four-inch drain.

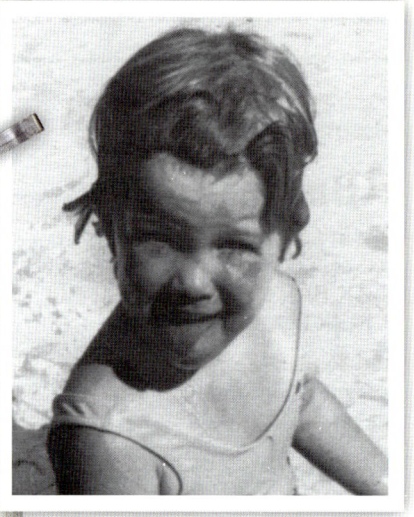

*Annie Arnoult*

*Emily Knapp*

Marion Burch: One summer we sat around and dreamed up a day camp. Four or five weeks later, we had 120 kids going crazy. The first day was drop-off and it was pouring. All the felt letters that we had ironed onto the kids' camp T-shirts—to identify and organize them—got drenched and fell off in the rain. We didn't know who anyone was or in which group they belonged! Of course, it worked out fine. All the kids had a blast and the counselors did, too.

Mike Caswell: One year, the swim team really needed new lane ropes. So, after a little fishing trip, I brought back one hundred pounds of shrimp. I catered a private party to raise the money for the lane ropes and I invited all the swim team families. I had a fabulous Zydeco band, and we had a big pot of boiling water right over by the pool. We cooked the shrimp outside there. I paid the waitstaff myself to help us out, because this was on a Monday, when the Club was closed.

**INFORMAL DINING**
12 Noon to 9 p.m.
TUES. — SAT.
12 Noon to 3 p.m. SUN.

Available Now
All Food Available Except Flaming Dishes
PLEASE MAKE RESERVATIONS
El Patio "Poolside" — 622-3667

**EVERY WEDNESDAY**
PLANTATION BUFFET DINNER
(Informal Dining in Patio Room)

**BY SPECIAL DEMAND**
EVERY SATURDAY —
Spaghetti With all Kinds of Sauce
Served With a Glass of Wine
$5.75* — Children $3.50
We Fix — You Match Served With
Garlic Bread, Green Salad
Served in the Patio Room
6:00 p.m.
RESERVATIONS 622-3667
ONLY $5.75* plus Tax and Gratuity
Dress Casual
This is a promise of a fun-filled evening
— Invite your friends.
SPAGHETTI NIGHT
ALSO — FRIDAY NIGHT SPECIAL
Check When Making Your Reservations — 622-3667

Jeff Cross: Back in the eighties, there was this huge demand for casual dining. People said they didn't want to eat in some dreary old low-ceilinged dining room and that's why they weren't going to eat at The Briar Club. So we thought, Okay, let's build the family locker rooms in the original tennis building. We took the locker rooms out from where they were and turned the area into a casual dining area.

Then people said that we couldn't possibly have the casual dining room here when the kitchen is way the heck down at the other end of the property. So someone had the thought of putting a kitchen adjacent to the new dining room, and I thought, What? We're going to have two kitchen staffs, two chefs? But they forged full speed ahead.

Mark Worscheh: In the late eighties, the Club found itself without a manager. Hans Kohler left. The Board undertook a search, but in the meantime, the Club was without a manager. My father, Erik Worscheh, had been manager of the Petroleum Club for many years and had retired. They called him up, and he served as interim manager for about six months until Miguel Olmedo was hired.

# Tennis is On!

Randy Burch: Johnny Perez was the Club pro in the eighties. At the time, we had a group of A players who didn't like Johnny. The A players just took everything. They didn't like C players on the court, didn't even like watching. We had two courts then, added courts three and four. From two to four on Sunday afternoon, Johnny gave the courts to the C players for doubles games. He gave us lesser players something to hang onto. He supported the less talented (but equally intense) players. I've been playing with Fred Carpenter and Page Piland since then, since the early 1970s.

Eleanor Beebe: Johnny Perez was a city employee who gave tennis lessons at Pumpkin Park. Every Thursday morning, he would come to The Briar Club and give ladies lessons. When Mike Doty first arrived in 1983, Tracy Glass and I were at Johnny's class. We decided to introduce ourselves to Mike and invite him to hit with us. Much to our surprise, he did! Mike told us that he had great plans for the Club, and that we would soon have a league.

Mike implemented every important facet of the tennis program that exists today. With the help of the Tennis Committee, he organized the First Briar Club Pro-Am Classic on the weekend of October 9–11, 1986, and it was a Club-wide tennis festival. In subsequent years, the Pro-Am included Calcutta parties, tennis three-ring circus activities for the juniors, formal and informal dances, raffles, and exhibitions. At first, only the top-level players could play, but eventually everyone was paired with a local pro.

Mike encouraged a group of us to form a Houston Ladies Tennis Association citywide league team. There are now six HLTA teams at The Briar Club. The first team was the C-1 Green Aces. He also instituted a very active junior program, and George Schuldberg, the assistant pro, was a very popular teacher. George was witty and played in a rock band—the kids found him super-cool, and would proudly show his autograph on the sides of their sneakers.

---

**The 1st Annual Briar Cup Championship Tennis Tournament**

Saturday, March 15th - 8:00 A.M.
Entry Fee: $15.00 Per Person
Includes: Lunch, Awards and Specially Designed T-Shirt

We will have ball boys and linesmen for the finals

Award Ceremony starts at 7:00 P.M. followed by a Cook Out

**MENU**

| | |
|---|---|
| Hamburger | $4.75 |
| Cheeseburger | $5.25 |
| Broiled Chicken Breast | $6.75 |
| Steaks: | $9.95 |
| N.Y. Strip | $9.95 |
| Rib Eye | $9.95 |
| T-Bone | $9.95 |
| Beef-ka-bob | $8.50 |

Above orders include a small salad bar
Cash bar
Dancing, Dancing, Dancing
To the 50's & Motown
Tennis Attire A Must
RSVP: 622-3667

---

## Tennis

**THE BRIAR CLUB MEXICO TENNIS TRIP PRO AM 1986** Las Hadas Resort
Manzanillo, Mexico
$495.00 per member.
Ask Mike for more details.

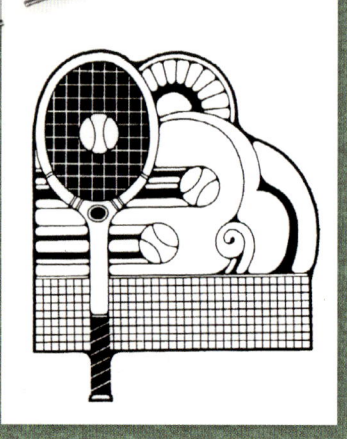

*First Wednesday night Ladies League. Back row: Mike Doty and Gaynor Gaston. Middle row: Maureen Suelau, Sue White, Nano Cox, and Betsy Earthman. Front row: Nancy Doty, Eleanor Beebe, Nancy Allen, Tracy Glass, and Tina Reese.*

*First Briar Club HLTA team, the C-1 Green Aces, 1984. Back row: Missa Sutton, Sally Tarlton, Nancy Allen, Sandy Turner, and Tina Reese. Front Row: Ann Mason, Shirley Horan, and Eleanor Beebe.*

*Junior Program, 1987*

*Sandy Turner and Nancy Allen, 1985*

## Tennis Circus

**Friday Evening**
October 9, 1987

| Ball Machine and Targets | Serve BLINDFOLDED | Play the Pros |

6:00 p.m. - 6:30 p.m.  
Win tickets for 25 junior prizes  
**KIDS**  
14 and under  
Raffle Prizes  
will be given away at 7:15 p.m.

Ringmasters  
Frank and Sue White

6:30 p.m. - 7:15 p.m.  
Win tickets for 50 adult prizes  
**ADULTS**  
Raffle Prizes  
will be given away at 9:00 p.m.

Prizes include racquets, dinners for two, tote bags, tennis lesson, clothing, gift certificates, etc., etc.

*Tennis Circus Pro-Am, 1987: Eleanor Beebe and George Schuldberg (assistant pro)*

56

*Briar Ladies Tennis Association officers, 1986: Sue White, Eleanor Beebe, Mike Doty, Nancy Allen, Tracy Glass, Sandy Turner, and Missa Sutton.*

*Nano Cox and Betsy Earthman, 1988*

*Scott Cook, Alex Jackson, Paul Beebe, and Andy Krusen*

*Alex Triantaphillis, 1986*

Wayne Bardwell: The year started out with great expectations and optimism. 1986 was the year that we decided to do major re-planning and overhauling of the Club. The board hired an architect to give us some preliminary ideas. Not far into the year, however, we began to realize that the Club was going to suffer financially due to the increasingly troublesome downturn in the Houston oil industry. We filed away the preliminary plans. During the year of 1986, the Club lost approximately 150 members with few replacement members. It was a tough year in every way but obviously the Club survived and prospered to become what it is today.

*Tony and Debbie Padon, rehearsal dinner, 1984*

# B

*Inside Playdeck*

*Frank, Mark, and Matthew Padon, 1984*

*Kelly, Scott Martin, Karen Kin, William Rabson, Marion Burch, and James Doyle*

# Chapter 5

**JITTERBUG LESSONS AND DANCE**

Friday, May 6th, 1994

Lessons from 7:00 p.m. - 9:00 p.m.
with Professional Dance Instructors

Dance with Live Band from 9:00 p.m. – Midnight

Heavy hors d'oeuvre buffet

Host Committee:
- Majorie & Palmer Hutcheson
- Susan & Sanford Criner
- Robin & Danny Klaes
- Lee & Bill Evans
- Jerrie & Peter Powell

**$15.00++ per person** (beer and wine included)

BRING YOUR PROSPECTIVE MEMBERS AS GUESTS!

Babysitting Available Upon Request.

---

CLIP AND SAVE

**BRIAR LADIES LUNCHEON**

March 9, 1994
Beginning at 10:30 a.m.

**WAYNE DOLCEFINO**

13 Undercover Investigator

Menu:
Mixed Field of Greens
with Tomato Vinaigrette
Trout Almondine
with Lemon Butter Sauce
Rice with Spinach and Walnuts
Corn Stuffed Tomato
Key Lime Pie

Reservations: 622-3667
24 hour cancellation required

CLIP AND SAVE

# The 1990s

Operation Desert Storm was initiated on January 16, 1991. In coming years, United States troops were posted to Somalia, Haiti, Bosnia, and Yugoslavia. At home, the growth of the World Wide Web was nothing short of phenomenal. Computers evolved from luxury items to basic necessities, and the Internet tied together all parts of the globe. Video games became the pastime du jour for American youth.

In Houston, President Bush held the world's Economic Summit at Rice University. The last Sakowitz store shut its doors. Kathy Whitmire ran for a record sixth term as mayor (she was defeated by Bob Lanier). Bob McNair declared that he would bring a national football franchise back to Houston.

During the 1990s, national attention turned to health and nutrition. The Briar Club surged into this fitness era by hiring Cederick Johnson to develop an attractive program for our members. Cederick had been a star running back for Rice University and had run the fitness program for the Houston Police Department. As his program grew, the Club added several additional trainers. The Briar Club was at the right place at the right time, and its fitness program continues to be the envy of Houston.

Fisher Trigg remembered the back wall problem, noting that the Club had a survey made and discovered an error in the south line facing the Park St. John condos. To correct this, an attractive brick wall was built to replace the old wire fence, and the Club also landscaped the rear gate entrance, adding a fountain and garden. This became the main entrance for the pool and fitness crowd.

The Briar Ladies Association continued to be an active and a vibrant part of Club life, thanks to the leadership of Dorothy Porter and Norma Pitrucha. The ladies made annual contributions to the Club, including beautiful silver serving pieces.

In their enthusiasm to swim, Nano Cox and Myron Steves were often observed climbing over the fence to the pool when it was closed. And, ever diligent, Mike Caswell had been seen jumping into the family pool with his clothes on if he spotted a child in trouble.

In 1993, Jay Grubb was president, AGAIN. "Word is, you have to do it until you do it right."

**PRESIDENTS**
| | |
|---|---|
| 1990 | James P. Hodges |
| 1991 | Cletus P. Dodd |
| 1992 | William T. Evans |
| 1993 | Jay C. Grubb |
| 1994 | Richard E. C. Miller |
| 1995 | John E. McDonald |
| 1996 | Michael L. Caswell |
| 1997 | Fisher Trigg |
| 1998 | Timothy McDaniel |
| 1999 | John Neighbors |

*Barbara Beich:* The snack bar had rubber matting and you'd come in wet off the grass—muddy, wet, grassy feet all over. The booths had springs sticking out and you'd sit and go boing. The kids loved it. There'd be ketchup all over the floor, on the rubber mats, and everybody was barefoot, and the kids went wild. And the food was greasy hamburgers. They used to fry everything.

The snack bar was awesome. The kids were so happy.

*Nancy Guest:* We loved that hamburger shack. It had booths like from *Happy Days*. That's where you got your food. Everybody ate hamburgers and hot dogs. We sat at banquettes with laminate tables. It was perfect.

Mike Caswell: I had to get used rental equipment to open the first fitness center. The two of us—Russell Worley and myself—did the inspections necessary to put in the exercise facility. We nearly got run out of town because people said, "There's no cash flow!"

I said, "We need to build the facility to increase the members—that's how it cash-flows."

And that's what happened.

There was a lot of turmoil about what to build, what not to build. I always said, "Build it and they will come. Build it and the cash will flow."

## FITNESS

### AEROBIC CLASSES

**\*STEP REEBOK:**
  Mon.-Wed.-Fri. 8:00-9:00 a.m.
  Tue.-Thur. 5:30-6:30 p.m.

**POWER SCULPT:**
  Tue.-Thur. 8:00-9:00 a.m.

**\*WATER AEROBICS:** Begins May 2nd
  Mon.-Wed.-Fri. 9:00-10:00 a.m.
  \*(Weather permitting)

\* If interested in the 8:00 a.m. Step Class, please call Tina before coming! 622-3667, ext. 247.

### COST FOR AEROBIC CLASSES

$30/month (unlimited) .................. $5.00/class
$45/month (unlimited non-member) ..... $8.00/class

### KARATE CLASSES

When:  TUESDAYS
Place:  Fitness Center
Ages:  6-18
Cost:  $60.00 / month
Contact Tina at 622-3667, ext. 247

\*Once you have attended a class you will be enrolled for a month of Karate regardless of vacations, sickness, etc.

### HEALTH AND FITNESS NEWS

**The Lean Green Nutrition Machine**

Yes, there is such a thing as health food, and it's name is broccoli. One serving of fresh broccoli (one cup, chopped) gives you about 90% of your daily requirement of vitamin A (in the form of beta carotene), 200% of Vitamin C, 6% niacin, 10% calcium, 10% of thiamin, 10% of phosphorus, and 8% iron. It is also rich in potassium and has 5 grams of protein. Wait, there's more. One serving provides about 25% of your daily fiber needs — a critical area in which the American diet is usually deficient. Moreover, studies have found that broccoli is one of the vegetables that may protect against certain forms of cancer. All this and only 45 calories.

### NEW! GROUP SWIM LESSON PROGRAM

**You Get Four 45 Minute Lessons For $60.00**

First Session Starts May 7th through May 28th

Second Session Starts June 4th through June 25th

Group I Beginners - 9:00 a.m. - 9:45 a.m.
Group II Advanced Beginners - 9:45 a.m. - 10:30 a.m.
Group III Intermediate - 10:30 a.m. - 11:15 a.m.
Group IV Advanced / Swimmer 11:15 a.m. - 12 noon

Contact Tina at 622-3667, ext. 247 to Sign-Up.

### ATTENTION MEMBERS: FITNESS CENTER EXPANSION

Keeping up with the wishes of the membership and with growing trends for a better fitness facility and exercise equipment, the Board of Directors has approved the expenditure for fitness center expansion. The work will consist of enclosing the roofed area of the upper deck and the purchasing of several state of the art Cybex and cardio vascular equipment. The work is targeted for completion this summer. We apologize for any inconvenience this may cause in your daily use of this facility during this work. Please supervise your children by not allowing them in the upper deck during construction.

Thank you very much, The Board of Directors of the Briar Club

*"Your Opinions at Work!"*

Mike Caswell: Swim team was so fun every kid around wanted to join. From about 1985 on we've had outstanding swim teams here at The Briar Club. Every spring, we had a banquet for all the swim team clubs to get a schedule together and see if there were any conflicts. Houston, Lakeside, River Oaks, Forest Club… It was in the late eighties, and it was The Briar Club's turn to host. At one point, the Lakeside coach—I called him the Lost Kid of Summer—was appointed by the other clubs to tell me the bad news, that it wasn't fair for us to win all the time, and that we'd have to split our team into two.

And I said, "Great idea! Wonderful idea. We're going to kick your ass twice now, and the championship will be here at The Briar Club between our own two teams!"

This was everything we wanted. See, we just had too many kids—over two hundred of them—and most of them didn't get to swim in the first heat, which was the one that counts. So, that summer onward, we had a Red Team and a Black Team.

## SWIMMING PROGRAM

### 1994 SWIM TEAM

For the 20th consecutive year, the Briar Club Swim Team returns as the only undefeated team in the Country Club League. The tradition continues as Head Coach David Houston and his staff carry on the winning ways and prepare for another successful season. Due to an expected large number of swimmers, the Country Club League has requested the Briar Club provide a more comparable team in size as other Clubs. Therefore, in order to remain in the League, this year's Swim Team will be divided in two teams picked arbitrarily by the coaches and will compete at different times. However, both teams will practice together as shown below. Be a part of the winning teams and suit up for this year's Briar Club Swim Team. This program is restricted to **members only.** Cost is $95.00 plus tax.

### PRACTICE SCHEDULE

During School Year, Practice Begins: Monday, May 16th; Time: 8-under 3:30-4:15 p.m., 9-over 4:15-5:00 p.m. Morning Practice Begins: Tuesday, May 31st; Time: 6-under & 11-over 9:00-10:00 a.m.; 7-8 years old 10:00-11:00 a.m.; 9-10 years old 11:00-12:00 p.m. Note: Afternoon practice will continue for swimmers with morning conflicts on Monday, Wednesdays and Fridays 4:30 -5:30 p.m.

### PRE SEASON SWIM TEAM WORKOUT

The swim team expands it's season by offering a 4 week pre swim team program on Mondays and Wednesdays from 4:00 - 5:00 p.m. Tina Peacock will concentrate on instruction and stroke production. Date: April 18 - May 11, Cost: $45.00, For twice a week, and $30.00 for once a week.

### SWIM TEAM TUNE-UP CLINICS

Advance Clinic: (Must have prior swim team experience.) Date: May 7th, Time: 9:00 - 10:30 a.m., Cost: $20.00. Beginner Clinic: (For those not sure if they're ready for swim team, only know one stroke, or have inefficent breathing skills.) Date - May 14th, Time: 9:00 - 10:30 a.m., Cost: $20.00. MUST MAKE RESERVATIONS FOR BOTH CLINICS - CALL 622-7729

### POST SEASON SWIMMING PROGRAM

After the swim team is over, the swim staff will be offering 6 separate weeks of workouts and fun for ages 6-14. This program is designed to offer the best instructions with a low student/teacher ratio. This extended swim program will be a weekly program to meet your demanding summer schedule. The swim program schedule will meet Monday - Friday, twice a day (11:00 a.m. -12:00 p.m. and 3:00 p.m. - 4:00 p.m.) Swimmers may only attend one of the two workouts each day. Cost: $30.00 + tax / week. Program Dates: Week 1—July 5-8, Week 2—July 11-15, Week 3—July 18-22, Week 4—July 25-29, Week 5—August 1-5, Week 6—August 8-12

### SWIMMING LESSONS

30 Minutes Per Lesson; Private $20.00, Semi-Private - $15.00; Group of 3 to 4 students - $12.00; Classes Available for: Beginner, Intermediate, and Advanced swimmers.

### SPRING BOARD DIVING LESSONS

Date: Starts — Monday, June 6th; Time: 8:00 - 9:00 a.m.; Time: Monday, Wednesday, and Friday. Instructor —Nonnie Kaposta: Nonnie has competed internationally for many years and participated in the 1980 & 1984 Olympics. She was also an NCAA All-American diver for the University of Houston. Note: Lessons are $12.00 an hour with a minimum of three lessons. The full amount of $36.00 is due on the first day of lessons. Sign up at the Pro-Shop or call 622-7729.

Barbara Beich: They had so many kids, they had two-a-day practices, and I brought my kids to both to wear them out! We would go in the morning, come home for lunch and a nap, and then go back in the late afternoon. Bentley one year won the pillow award, for spending so much time here with the swim team.

There was a big lawn here, all grassy, just outside the lounge. After a day of wet kids, it was all muddy, so before heading home, we'd have the kids jump into the pool to clean off the grass and dirt.

Don't tell.

Did they shock the pool every single night?

Mike Caswell: The immediate past Board president was chairman of the Long-Range Planning Committee. He provided a smooth connection between the Board and the Committee. He understood the Club inside and out.

We actually did things in an orderly fashion in those days, but it was impossible trying to convince people to do this or that. They'd be dug in. Some people didn't want to change one trashcan.

So the Committee got frustrated, and I said, "What we really need on this Committee is a woman." Of course, there's Dorothy Porter sitting a few seats down from me. So the room got real quiet for a minute, until Dorothy said, "Well, what am I? Chopped liver?" And I said, "Hell no, Dorothy, you're one of the guys!"

*Dorothy Porter and Jay and Joanna Grubb. Dorothy and Jay are the only two to serve as president twice.*

*Mike and Barbara Caswell*

John Neighbors: The major renovations were finalized during my year as president. That was a highlight—all this, the interior of the former lanai, the President's Room, and the Terrace Rooms. As far as any other major incidents that year, no explosions, no fires, nobody went to jail. It was kind of boring.

## CLUB NO MINORS
Opens at 5:00 p.m. on Saturday and Sundays
Bartender and Food Service on Upper Deck. (21 and over)

Barbara Caswell: After we did the bathroom re-do, The Briar Club hired Cynthia Stone and Russell Worley to redesign the Clubhouse. They did the floating ceiling thing. The ceilings were so low it was difficult to make something aesthetic. This is an old house, basically, and any time you go fussing with the ceiling you start breaking pipes, and it's a mess and a mistake. The year Cynthia Stone put all that in, she got the top four design awards in the city.

Just after all the construction, the manager said to me, "Mrs. Caswell, would you help us redecorate the new bathrooms and locker rooms?" I said, "Sure, happy to help." They were just fixing to do the workout rooms upstairs. Well I didn't know what I was doing. So we went downtown and picked out some real pretty wallpaper and it looked great!

But you know, then the next person comes along, and the design tastes change. Everybody brings their own ideas. Things change. The Club looks fabulous now. It's so sophisticated. And, it was fabulous to us then.

It's so important to know what came before, so you can better appreciate where you are now.

# Kids Club

ABC 123

# Bayou Bash/Shrimp Peel

67

# Chapter 6

Angela Bower's birthday, 2008

Sharon and Richard Lareau, Nancy Pustka, Evelyn Lareau, and David Pustka

Martha Cancelmo and Cynthia Kinney

Macy and Lindsay Wheeler, 2008

# The 2000s

The early years of the new millennium were eclipsed by shock and anxiety surrounding 9/11 and the Iraq War. America suddenly felt vulnerable within a world of global terrorism. National security became the prevailing priority, and security on a local level took on new proportions. The Briar Club hired security guards for its gates and parking lot. These men and women, matching vigilance with warm smiles, were instant favorites with all the members.

Tropical Storm Allison dropped thirty-seven inches of rain on Houston in 2001. In the following year, the Club offices were heavily damaged by a fire, which destroyed the bulk of Club records. In 2005, Hurricane Katrina brought thousands of evacuees to the city from New Orleans, some of whom became members of the Club. Only weeks later, Hurricane Rita made landfall near Sabine Pass. Threat of the storm triggered the largest urban evacuation in U.S. history. Then, on September 12, 2008, Hurricane Ike devastated the Houston metropolitan area. The Briar Club became a refuge for many families without power, and provided ice and fresh water to all affected.

**PRESIDENTS**
- 2000 Andrew Hero
- 2001 Ray Frierson
- 2002 Dorothy Porter
- 2003 L. Burke Windham
- 2004 Clay Lilienstern
- 2005 Nancy Putska
- 2006 R. Peyton Burch
- 2007 Paige Hagle
- 2008 Mark Worscheh
- 2009 Bill Wade

*Kyra Link and Andrea Horvath Link, 2000*

Jeff Cross: The Briar Club has weathered storms pretty well. We weathered Carla in 1961 and we weathered Alicia in '83 as well. Whenever there's an emergency, we go in and tell the bridge ladies it's time to move out, and they say "Let us finish this rubber."

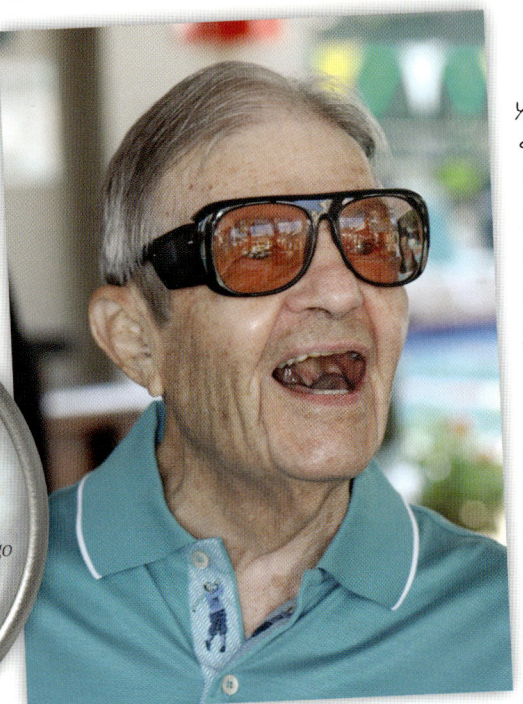

Rich Lareau: Let me tell you about Mr. Myron Steves on the occasion of Hurricane Rita. The nation's eyes were on Houston. Houston had emptied out. My family was waiting for me at home, in terror—I was going to evacuate everyone to Centerville. Well, I had just checked all the doors and windows in the Clubhouse for the fifth time, but I took a last walk through the campus to make sure I hadn't forgotten anything and moved the plants to safe places. Suddenly I saw this person out there at the back entrance, pulling and banging on the gates—and it was Myron. I think he was ninety-four years old at the time.

I said, "Myron, the sky is falling! Run for your life! We're evacuating!"

"I've come to swim," he shouted.

I said, "I dropped the water in the pool three feet."

And he said, "That's all right. I don't take much."

Mario Falfan was celebrated for twenty-two years of service. He started in housekeeping in 1985 under General Manager Hans Kohler. Years later, General Manager Miguel Olmedo promoted him to supervisor of housekeeping.

"When the people smile to me, talk to me, I keep it here in my heart.

"This Club is full of wonderful, wonderful people. They treated me well. They had respect for me. And some people, I feel, they loved me. The friendship was beautiful.

"Once we had a French chef—Chef Jacques. When he was leaving the Club, he called me into his office. He shook my hand and said, Thank you for your friendship, Mario. He gave me a box of French shaving cream and cologne. A wonderful man. I don't use it. I never opened a bottle. I just keep it near me.

"Mr. Richard Lareau is a marvelous, marvelous man. He calls me to his office one day and says, Mario, you are the age to rest. At home. He gave me a beautiful reception with a cake, a diploma, and a check from the Club."

*Richard Lareau, Mario Falfan, and Paige Hagle*

Rich Lareau: Club leaders had a vision. Members wanted the new Fitness Center to make a statement from an architectural perspective. They wanted the building to set a new standard that Briar Club members would expect in the future.

From the moment of our grand opening in January '05, it became evident we underestimated the amount of daily use. The increase in member participation was unexpected and significant.

We realized that the worst thing we could do that would quell the surge of enthusiasm would be to not fully service the needs and desires of our engaged membership. We knew that having an aesthetically beautiful building laid out to enhance ease of use, filled with the latest best-of-breed exercise and A/V equipment, was not enough to achieve our goal. It is the quality and amount of personal service delivered to our membership which elevates a first-rate fitness facility into a "first class" fitness experience.

Truly "first class" service encompasses complete and full service.

Being "full service" meant providing a quality fitness experience for the whole family.

Kevin Smith, the Club's director of fitness during this period, was instrumental in guiding the construction of the new facility and in ushering in the various new programs and services our members now enjoy. He once said, "We should all prepare ourselves to ride the wave of fitness enthusiasm throughout all areas of our Club."

What even Kevin wasn't expecting is that his wave of enthusiasm became a tidal tsunami of participation.

During these years, The Briar Club witnessed a dramatic transformation with the addition of the new Fitness Center. This state-of-the-art facility was so impressive that it changed the whole identity of the Club. No longer just for swimming, tennis, and dining, The Briar Club became an urbane fitness club with broad appeal and upscale operations. The new Fitness Center was immediately overwhelmed by member participation. Its design was nationally recognized, and it set the bar higher for fitness clubs across the country.

The old rec center was next in undergoing renovation. It became the Club's Wellness Center, the newest star on the campus and another indication of The Briar Club's commitment to staying ahead of the countrywide health curve. The family locker rooms were renovated and decorated under the direction of Club member Diane Josephs.

*John Johnston, Paige Hagle, Peter Petkas, Meg Tapp, Kevin Smith, Clay Lilienstern, Rich Lareau, Howard Cordray, Nancy Pustka, Mark Worscheh, Peyton Burch, Ron Schwartz, and Bill Rucker.*

Rhonda Barclay: Do you remember that little shop in the breezeway? I really loved that shop. It didn't have anything to do with anything. It didn't sell swimming or tennis gear. It was just an experiment. In fact, before the boutique, Mike Doty had his pro shop there, which made a kind of sense. I think there was still a little tennis stuff way in the back.

The shop used to be just left of the rec center door. They had jewelry, fancy clothing, skirts with slits in them… It lost money hand over fist. They had this girl running it who was a size zero, so she only brought in clothes in sizes zero, two, and four. And then she'd say, "I can order you a twelve…" And I'd say, "No thanks."

Jay Grubb: I remember the night we were trying to eat in the grille area and there wasn't a waiter to be found. There were no waiters anywhere. I said, "Where is everybody?" They were all outside standing by the back pool. There was a nude woman up in the condos talking on the phone by the window. Had about fifteen waiters there and none in the grille.

Paige Hagle: Really, The Briar Club changed my life. That's so cliché, but honestly it did. I'd been a working person, an attorney, and then we had this child and I said I'm going to stay at home with her. When we joined here, our daughter was one year old. I started playing tennis. I got into a Tuesday morning Club league. It was such an outlet for me. Here was my time with adults. It was really life-changing. The course of my life would have been different if I hadn't joined The Briar Club.

Barbara Beich: It just makes my heart sing to see my friends' kids here, grown now and with their own children. I saw Brian Caswell the other day on the side of the pool. I said, "Brian, I am so proud of you not hanging over your children during their swim lesson! Now they may even learn how to swim!"

Our kids have such wonderful memories. They'll never let us drop the membership.

Myron Steves: I won a blue ribbon for an exhibition lap at the twenty-five-meter freestyle meet here in 2004. I swam one length of the pool. There were all these kids cheering me on from the sides. They were very young, and they were all jumping and *ooh*ing and *aah*ing, saying "He's ninety years old! And he can still swim!"

*Myron Steves's ninety-fifth birthday, 2007*

Rich Lareau: There were significant pest problems here when I arrived. I called the exterminators and said, "I want the nuclear option."

I went to the highest level of attack. Not monthly, not weekly—DAILY.

We were simply not going to have a pest problem here. And, we haven't had evidence of pests in the neighborhood for a long time (Jay Grubb adds, "with more than two legs").

**Rich Lareau:** One day, a lady came up to me and said, "Are you going to put green dye in the pool for St. Patrick's Day?" And I said, "No, we're going to turn off the chlorine for five days beforehand."

Peter Petkas, an avid swimmer and champion of upgrading the heating of the Club's pools, was elected to the Board, supported by members who used the slogan: IF YOU LIKE THE HEATER, VOTE FOR PETER!

If you like the HEATER then vote for PETER !
Petkas for Briar Club Board.
SWIMMING
Don't let your VOTE go down the drain.

**Pete Gibson:** Although I've been blind from birth, I have come to the Club to swim since I was six years old. It was Jessie Wilhite, the trainer, that got me into lifting weights. He showed me how to work the machines. That was in the old rec center. I liked it there. It had a cozy feel to it. There was great camaraderie.

The new Fitness Center is pretty nice. I go on the treadmill quite a bit. Jessie trained me for a long time until I got independent enough that I could do things on my own. He showed me a way to memorize where all the machines were. He got me oriented. I made notes on a little tape recorder until I really got it.

They're renovating the old fitness center now. Vince Baker called to give me a heads-up about the construction areas. I'll have to walk on the south side of the pool for a while. It's a little more cluttered on that side, if I remember. Just another little challenge, a little speed bump on the road to training.

**Jay Grubb:** Pete [Gibson] has been a member of The Briar Club for more than twenty years. He is a graduate of The St. John's School and Rice University, and he has worked in past years for IBM and Texaco in computer disciplines.

During all of the Club renovations in the nineties, Pete indicated that he would be ever so pleased when all was completed and they ceased moving furniture and equipment around. That said, the Briar staff always serves as escort for Pete when any need is apparent. Pete Gibson is a truly remarkable individual and a loyal Briar Club member.

**Rich Lareau:** This Club has a lot of unsung heroes. For instance, Mark Didway. The sun never shines on Mark Didway. He's been our night watchman here for over twenty years. Only the earliest swimmers know him. Mark is the one that discovered the fire of 2002. He's a unique individual. He bikes here each evening, and stays here all night long. We're indebted to people like that.

*Mark Didway*

Tom Kamrath: My mother, Jeannie Gonzales, lives in the Lamar Tower. At ninety-five, she is the *grande dame* of the luncheon crowd, so I've been back to The Briar Club several times. It looks great.

*Jeannie Gonzales*

Nancy Guest: It's different than when I joined thirty-eight years ago. It was just a little neighborhood club, but it's evolved into a really nice place to bring a friend. Before, you brought your kids for swimming and a hot dog, but now you can have a really nice occasion. We had my daughter's wedding reception here.

*Susan and Lee Hancock*

*Cidette Rice, Ann Keibler, and Macy Wheeler, Starfish 2007*

Mark Worscheh: I couldn't be happier being president this year. We've got a great Board and we've met all sorts of challenges. We've just completed renovation of the family locker rooms, and they're dazzling. Now we have the challenge of the second floor of the rec center. Can we redevelop that into a highly attractive, multi-use facility? Yes. This Club can do it.

*Rich Andrae: The newest arena in fitness is wellness. This is a trend toward movement training with an emphasis on adapting the body to the stresses of our environment. Wellness is comprehensive, making everything before it seem incomplete. The fitness of the future is not about how much iron you pump or how hard you work out, it's about helping your mind and body adapt to the inevitable effects of aging.*

*Mary and Stuart Hill, Leonard and Millie Wilson*

Barbara Beich: Yoga is still my favorite class. It's so peaceful. It's one of the oldest classes here and it's been moved around, from room to room, dining room, fitness room. No matter. Have mat, will travel.

*Rich Lareau:
I'm not unfit,
I'm de-conditioned!*

Peyton Burch: I can still remember the first time I walked through the door of The Briar Club, and I thought,

Wow

*Rich Andrae, Peter and Belle Petkas, and Hugh Zabriskie, 2008 Penguin Club winners*

**Burke and Jennifer Windham**

*Caitlin and Alma Wheat*

*Don and Carol Frisby*

Bob Frazier and Fred Carpenter

Tony Padon

John Rice, Shepherd Swope, Leonard Fox, and Nicholas Hazen

Lindsay Wheeler and Gina de Pamphilis, 2008

77

# Breakfast with the Easter Bunny

Jack Link

Grant Eudey

# HALLOWEEN

Kyra Link, 2000

Elizabeth Edmonds, Donavan & Julia Burke

Halloween mixer

# Christmas Breakfast with SANTA

Danielle Lurie

Jingle Bell mixer

Liz Geddings

Sarah Grant, Allison & Trent Burch, Wilson Grant

New Year's Eve

79

Alyson Franklin, Jordan Geibel, and Maddy Smith

Moonlight Madness

Jack Schubert and Joe Wheat

80

Clare Hewitt, Jordan Geibel, and Maggie Wilson

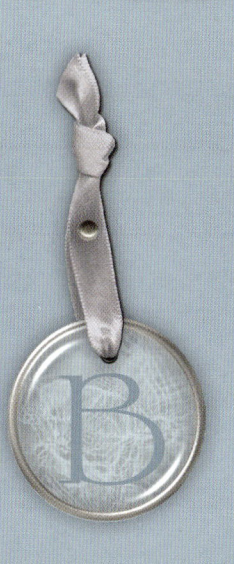

Coach Richard Butler and friends

81

# Father-Daughter Dance

*Jim and Allison Buaas*

*Peyton, Will, and Kallie Brown*

82

*Millie Sall, Judithe Little, and Leslie Ashby*

# Girls' Night Out

*Dixie Bowers, Paige Hagle, and Alma Wheat*

Mary and John Enerson

Janice and Jesse Luton, and Mildred and Wallace Ragan

Tammy and Dan Rogas

Eli and Jenifer Ben-Shoshan

Anthony and Maureen Rasche, and Mary and Stuart Hill

*Fall Party*

Greg and Janet Buffone, and Andy and Mary Boyd

Michael and Kim Grant, and Mark and Sue Worscheh

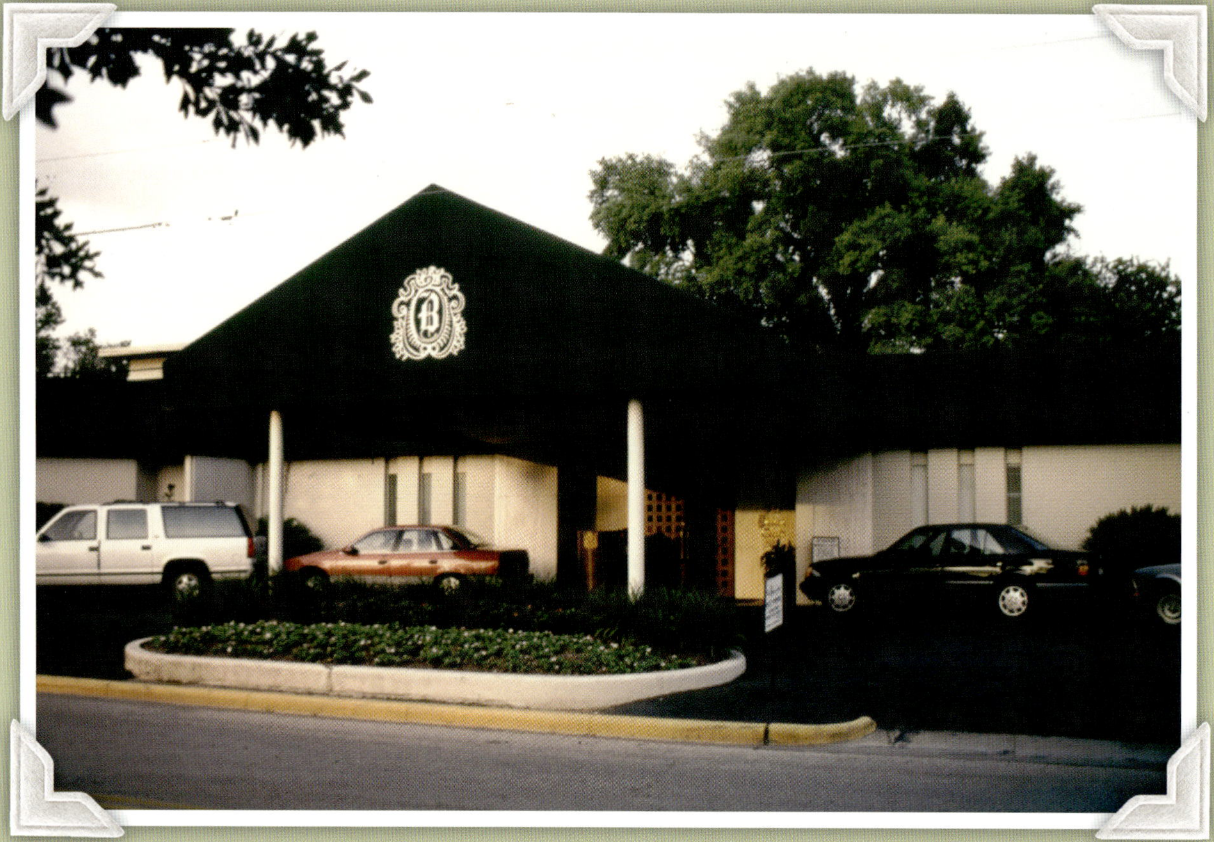

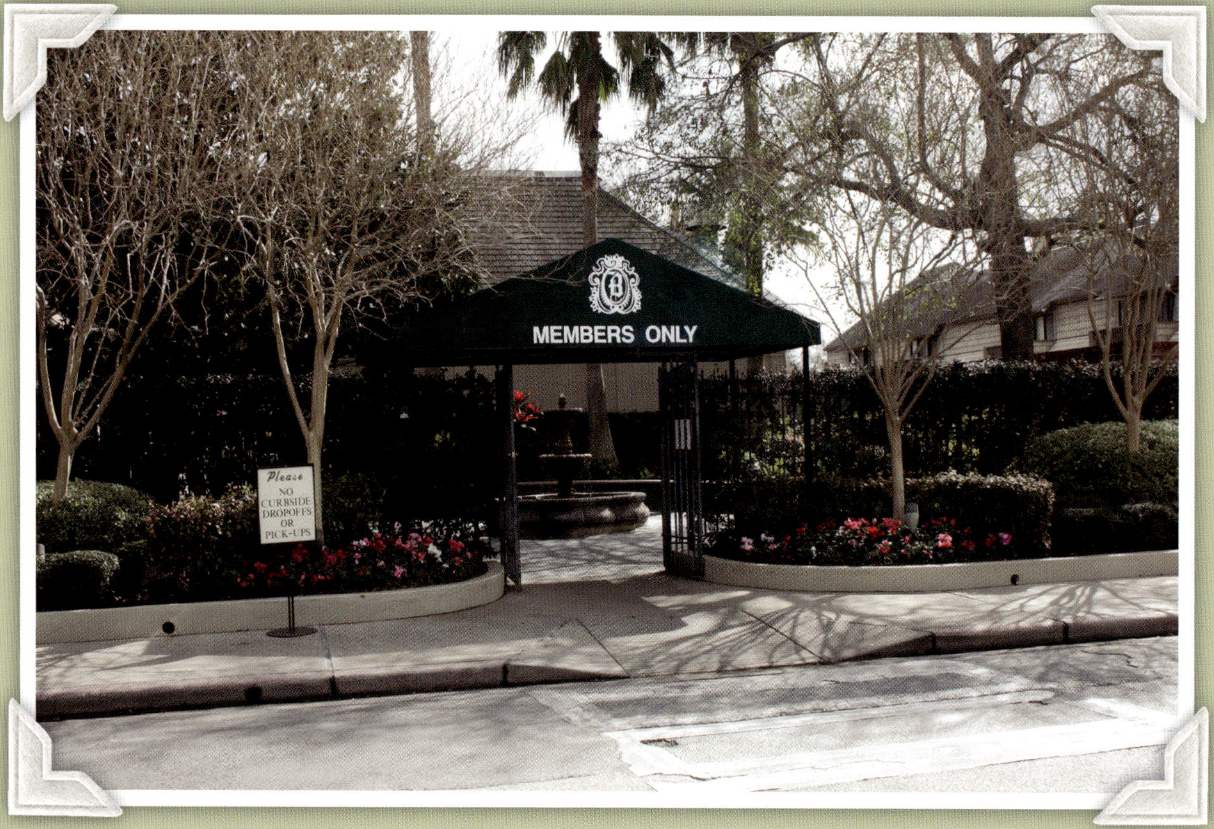
MEMBERS ONLY
Please
NO
CURBSIDE
DROPOFFS
OR
PICK-UPS

*Susu Ross, Mary Hill, and Shawn Greer*

*Peter Petkas, Garrett Kobs, and Jay Grubb*

## Our Staff

89

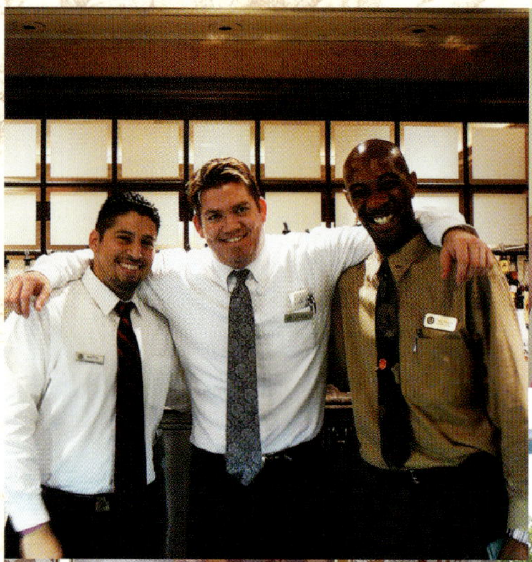
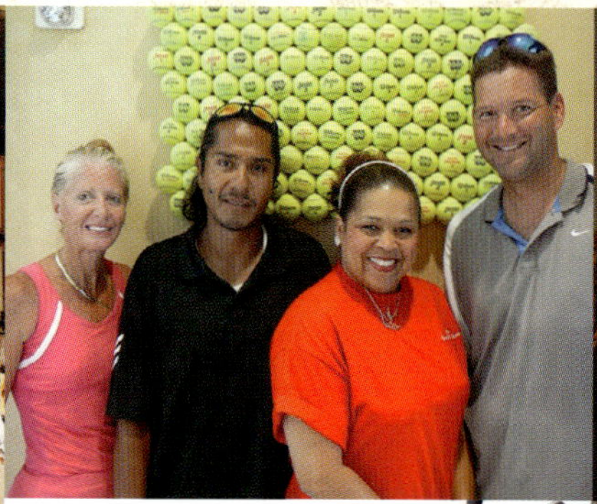
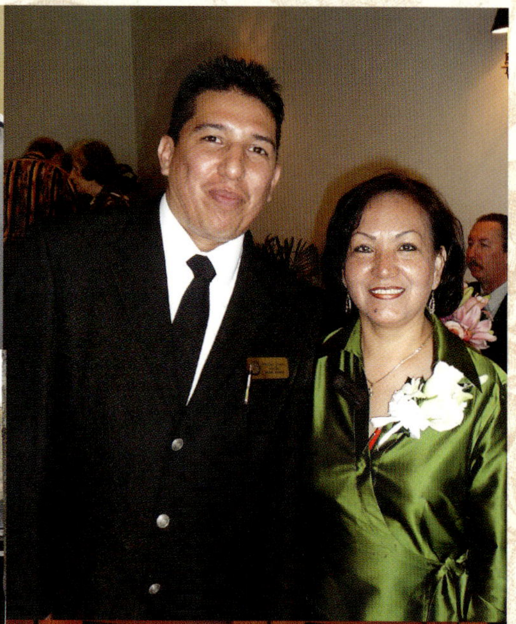
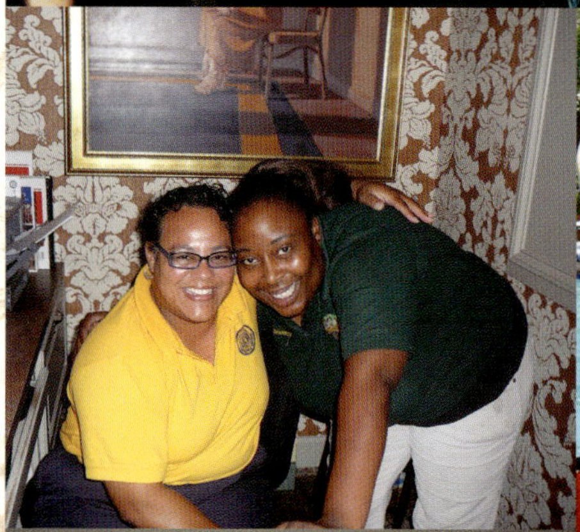
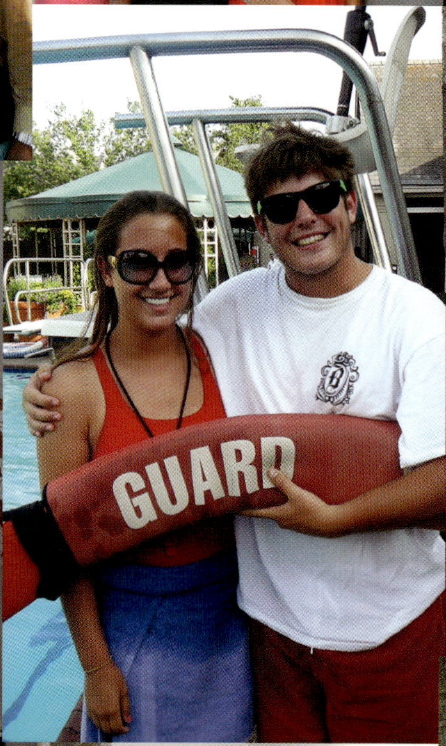
GUARD
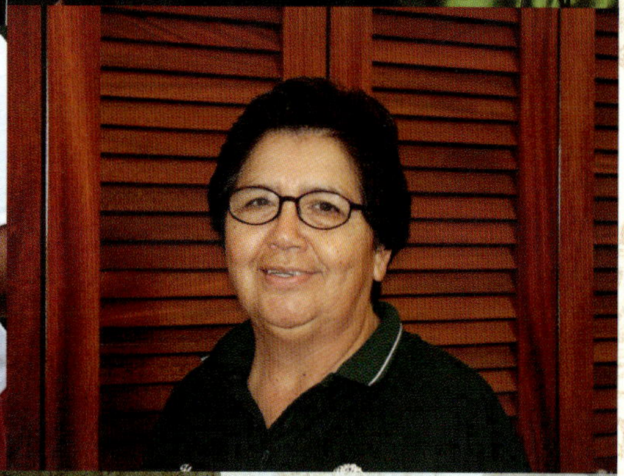
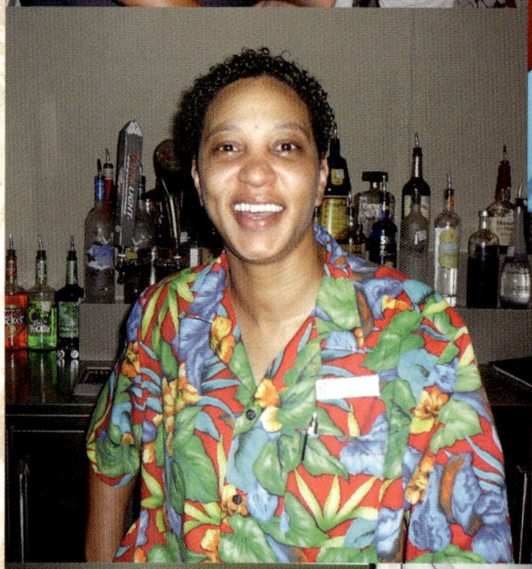
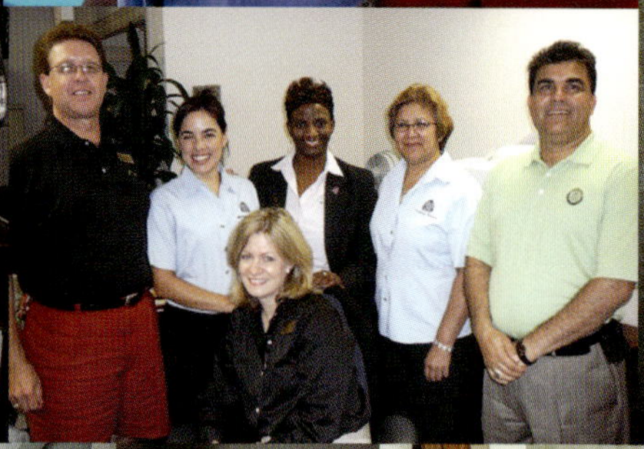
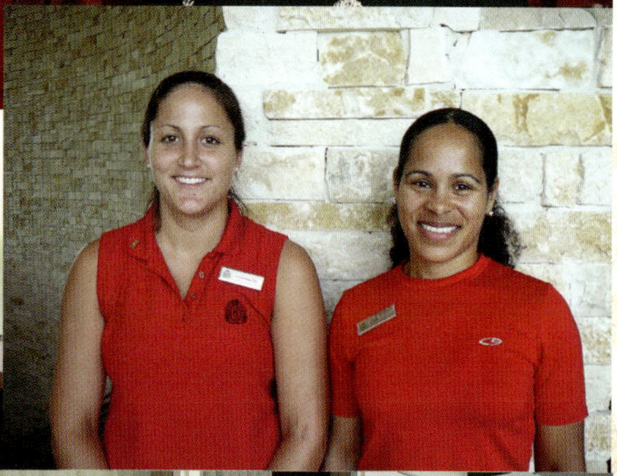
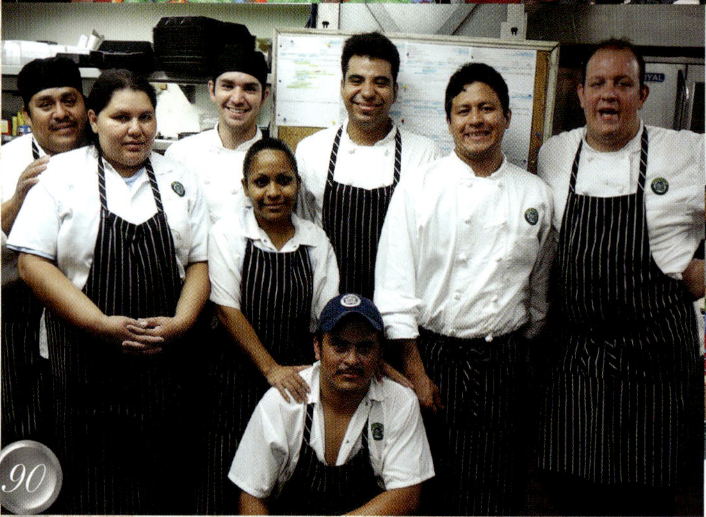
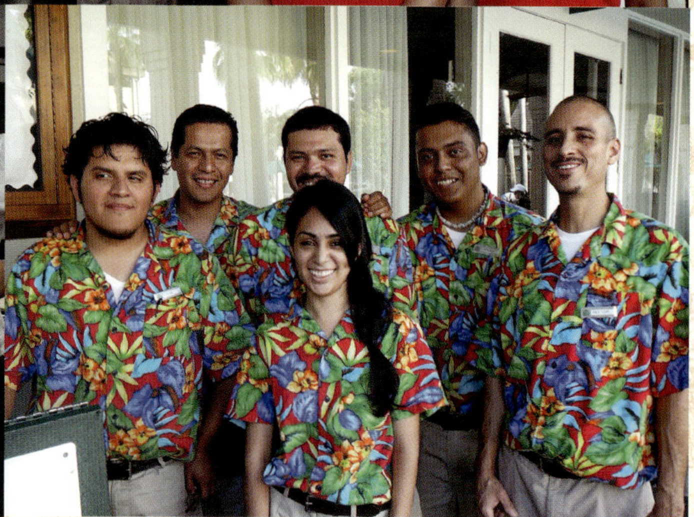

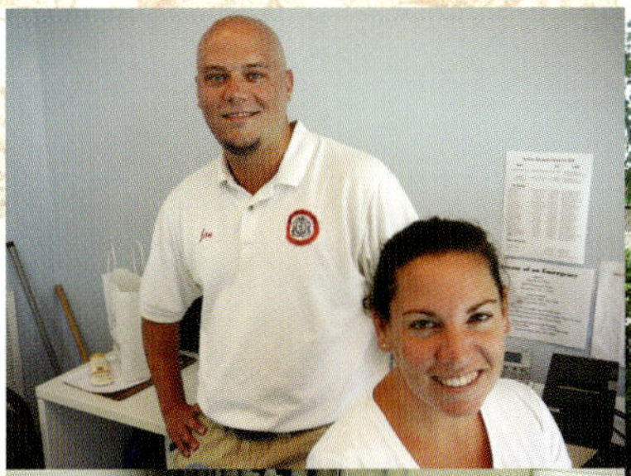
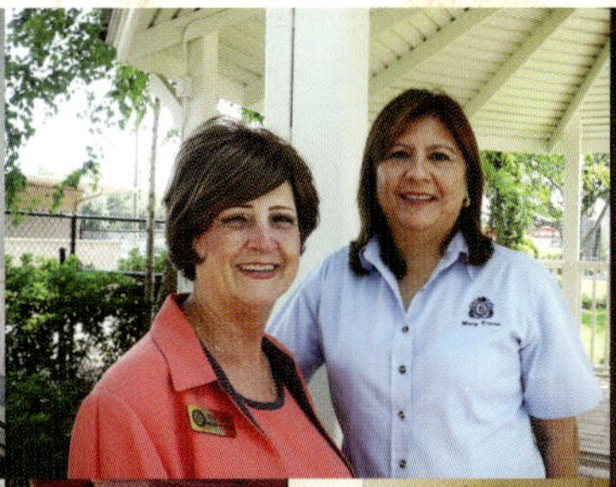
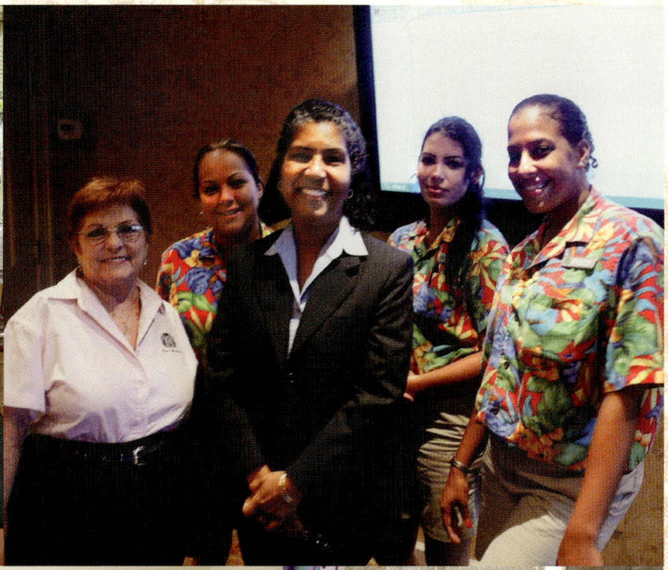
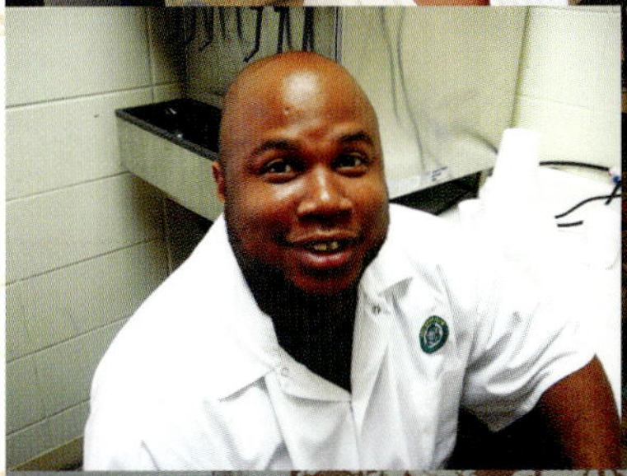
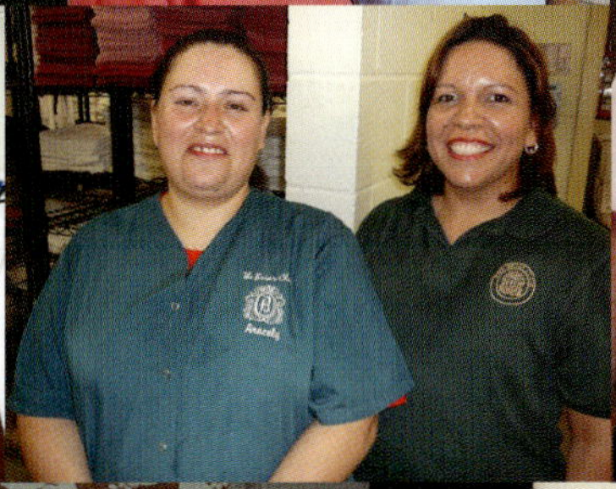
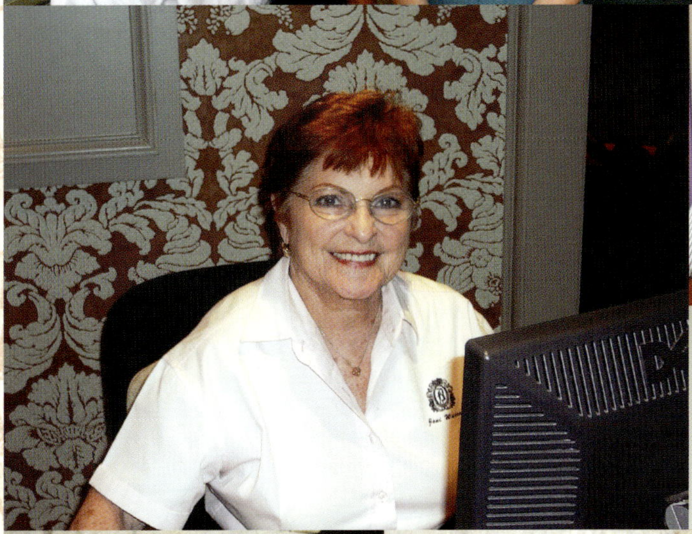
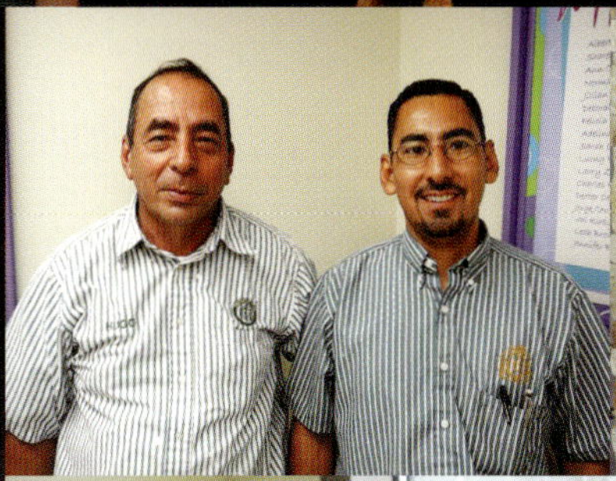
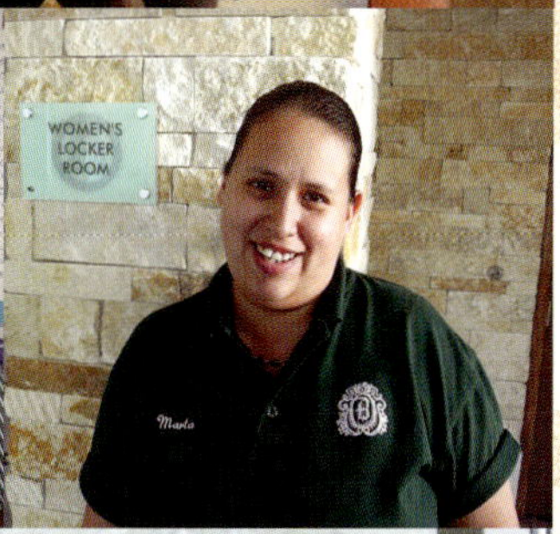
WOMEN'S LOCKER ROOM
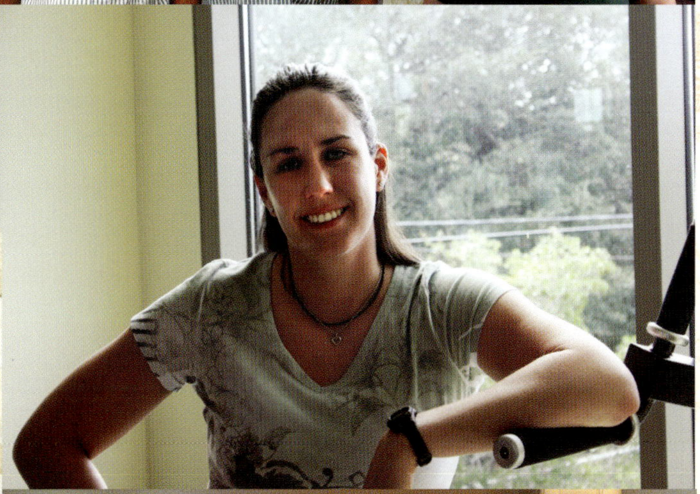
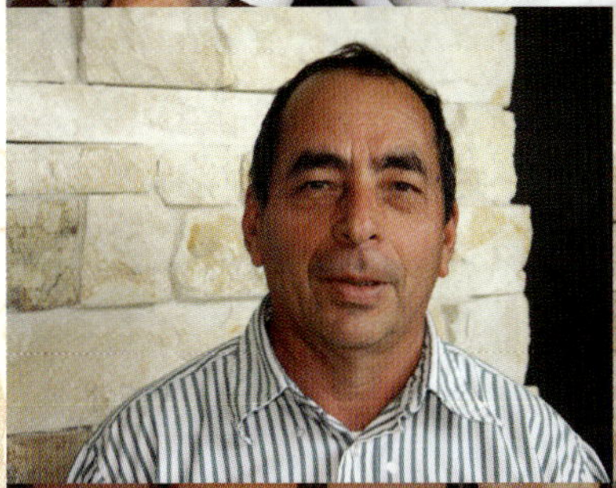
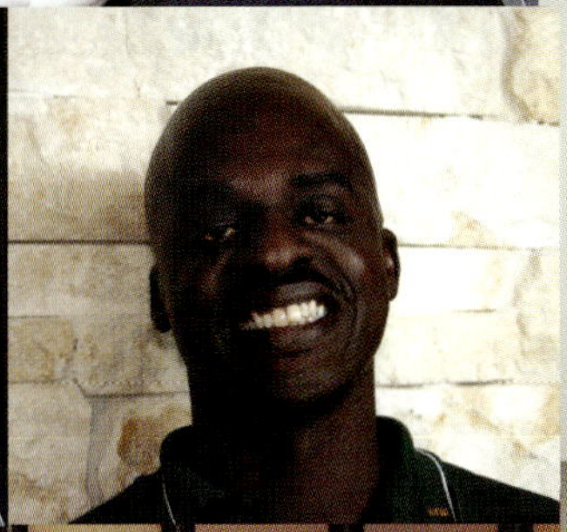
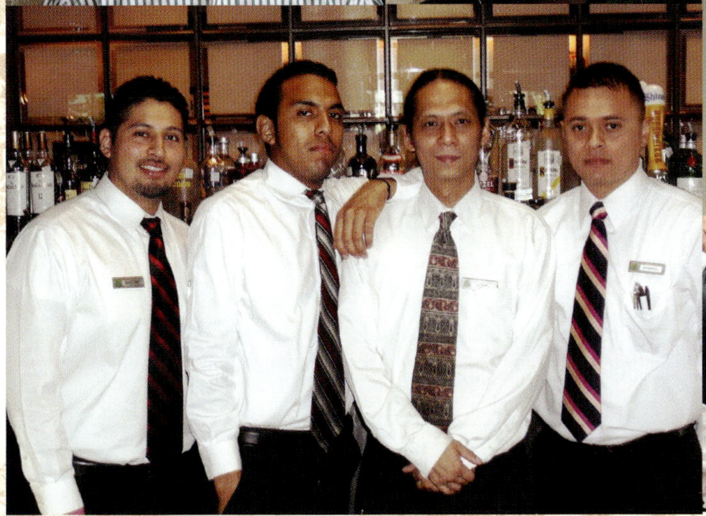
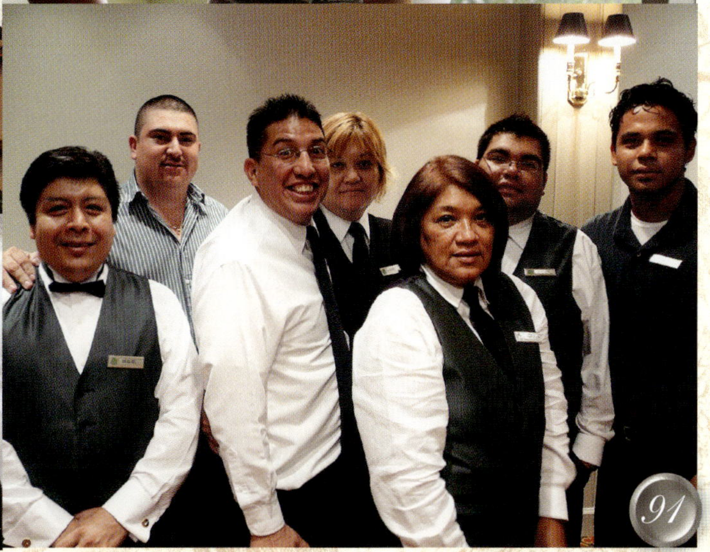

# Epilogue

Hurricane Ike photographed by the crew of ISS-17 aboard the International Space Station from a vantage point of 220 statute miles above Earth. Photo courtesy of NASA.

On September 12, 2008, Hurricane Ike devastated the Houston area. Ike was the third-largest hurricane ever to hit the United States. Its eye had a sixty-mile diameter and the size of its wind field was the largest ever recorded. The hurricane razed power lines, ripped up trees, and spawned tornados on its slow route up the Texas coast. In its wake, over four and a half million people were left without power.

The Briar Club suffered modest damage from Ike and was without power for only a few hours. Rich Lareau and members of his staff gathered on the campus to wrestle fallen fences into place. Elizabeth Griffin telephoned all elderly members to inquire about their safety and access to food and drinking water. Over the next week, waitstaff and fitness trainers brought meals to stranded members twice a day. The Club offered ice and bottled water at cost to all families. Chef Lance prepared lunches and dinners—dubbed the Hurricane Buffet—to accommodate hundreds of affected families, day after day.

People will talk about Hurricane Ike for decades, but perhaps the finest memory of this natural disaster was the compelling human triumph. The Briar Club showed a dedication to the well-being of its members, and to the preservation of their community. Rich Lareau led a staff of remarkable people in the speedy recovery of our grounds and our spirits. He recalled for us all the hopes and expectations of the Club's founding members—that this Club would be *more* than the sum of its membership. The Briar Club would be a community with a soul.

# Past Presidents

| | | | |
|---|---|---|---|
| 1950 | Warren P. Cunningham, Jr.* | 1982 | Fred F. Morgan, Jr. |
| 1951 | Gerald E. Veltmann* | 1983 | Fred A. Carpenter, Jr. |
| 1952 | Kraft W. Eidman* | 1984 | Thomas W. Gillette |
| 1953 | E. A. Smith* | 1985 | J. Stanley Taylor |
| 1954 | John C. Williams* | 1986 | C. Wayne Bardwell |
| 1955 | W. Kenneth Davis* | 1987 | Joffre J. Cross II |
| 1956 | Dr. J. M. Dougall* | 1988 | Dorothy M. Porter* |
| 1957 | Shelton W. Boyce, Jr.* | 1989 | Lee E. Hancock |
| 1958–59 | Zeke Tipton* | 1990 | James P. Hodges |
| 1960 | Ira W. Strickler* | 1991 | Cletus P. Dodd |
| 1961–62 | J. B. Ross* | 1992 | William T. Evans |
| 1963 | Sam Tigner* | 1993 | Jay C. Grubb |
| 1964 | Evert A. Rogers* | 1994 | Richard E. C. Miller |
| 1965 | Robroy C. Carroll* | 1995 | John E. McDonald |
| 1966 | Joffre J. Cross* | 1996 | Michael Caswell |
| 1967 | Lewis F. Sherer* | 1997 | Fisher Trigg |
| 1968 | H. E. Carrico, Jr.* | 1998 | Timothy McDaniel |
| 1969 | J. F. Freel | 1999 | John Neighbors |
| 1970 | W. Peter Lipscomb* | 2000 | Andrew Hero |
| 1971 | Lewis E. Brazelton* | 2001 | Ray Frierson |
| 1972 | Ben F. Chenault, Jr.* | 2002 | Dorothy M. Porter* |
| 1973 | Jay C. Grubb | 2003 | L. Burke Windham |
| 1974 | A. Fred Armstrong* | 2004 | Clay Lilienstern |
| 1975 | Glynn F. Martin* | 2005 | Nancy Putska |
| 1976 | A. T. Hubly, Jr.* | 2006 | R. Peyton Burch |
| 1977 | George G. Harris* | 2007 | Paige Hagle |
| 1978 | Herbert W. Varner* | 2008 | Mark Worscheh |
| 1979 | Arnold E. Stremmel* | 2009 | Bill Wade |
| 1980 | William W. Caldwell* | | |
| 1981 | George A. Donaldson | * Deceased | |

# Past Briar Ladies Presidents

| | | | |
|---|---|---|---|
| 1950 | Mrs. Miles Strickland | 1977 | Mrs. Wm. W. Caldwell |
| 1951 | Mrs. W. H. McKelvy | 1978 | Mrs. T. E. Thomas |
| 1952 | Mrs. Maurice Truitt | 1979 | Mrs. John N. Buckley |
| 1953 | Mrs. Wendell H. Hamrick | 1980 | Mrs. Jewell N. Higginbotham |
| 1954 | Mrs. Virgil Childress | 1981 | Mrs. W. Henry Colbert |
| 1955 | Mrs. Jack Abbott | 1982 | Mrs. C. Roy Pitrucha |
| 1956 | Mrs. Sheldon Boyce | 1983 | Mrs. James H. Barry |
| 1957 | Mrs. Jack Abbott | 1984 | Mrs. L. B. S. Porter |
| 1958 | Mrs. Jack Howeth | 1985 | Mrs. C. H. Graham |
| 1959 | Mrs. Ira Strickler | 1986 | Mrs. V. C. Bracher |
| 1960 | Mrs. Ray Nixon | 1987 | Mrs. C. K. Fierstone |
| 1961 | Mrs. Richard Powell | 1988 | Mrs. Frederick W. Kohlhausen |
| 1962 | Mrs. Frank Ashcraft | 1989 | Mrs. Stuart Hill & Mrs. C. Roy Pitrucha |
| 1963–64 | Mrs. Evert Rogers | | |
| 1965 | Mrs. Joffre Cross | 1990 | Mrs. Jewell N. Higginbotham |
| 1966 | Mrs. H. E. Carrico, Jr. | 1991 | Mrs. Clint Faulkner |
| 1967 | Mrs. John Buckley | 1992 | Mrs. L. B. S. Porter |
| 1968 | Mrs. W. Peter Lipscomb | 1993 | Ms. Peggy Taylor |
| 1969 | Mrs. Ed F. Heyne | 1994 | Mrs. James Hodges |
| 1970 | Mrs. C. K. Fierstone | 1995 | Mrs. C. Howard Graham |
| 1971 | Mrs. Marvin Damanzuk | 1996 | Mrs. Zelda Fierstone |
| 1972 | Mrs. Joseph M. Valenza | 1997 | Mrs. C. Howard Graham |
| 1973 | Mrs. Conrad Cady | 1998 | Mrs. Zelda Fierstone |
| 1974 | Mrs. Lawrence F. Athy | 1999–2001 | Briar Club Women's Association Committee |
| 1975 | Mrs. A. T. Hubly, Jr. | | |
| 1976 | Mrs. J. J. Campbell | | |

## Contributors to Book or Archives

We would like to thank all of the members, staff, and former employees who contributed stories, information, photos, and other memorabilia. Unfortunately, we were unable to use all of it in this book, but it will all be kept for posterity in the archives of the Club.

Rich Andrae — employee
Rhonda Barclay
Eleanor Beebe
Barbara Beich
Paula Porter Bohls
Peyton Burch
Randy & Elizabeth Burch
Fred Carpenter
Mike & Barbara Caswell
Al Chivers — former general manager
Marion Burch Cimbala
Jeff Cross
Nancy Cunningham
Mario Falfan — former employee
Don & Carol Frisby
Jeannette Clift George
Pete Gibson
Tom Gillette
Joanna Grubb
Nancy Guest
Paige Hagle
Susan Hancock
Jeannie Hero
Csilla Horvath
Cederick Johnson — former employee
Tom Kamrath — former employee
Faye Keeton
Adrianne Atchley Kipp
Tony & Debbie Padon
Norma Pitrucha
Sherry Schnapp — employee
Virginia Schneider
Alphonse Sims — employee
Mary Lou Soper
Myron Steves
Fisher Trigg
Tasso Triantaphyllis
Jan Vick — employee
Lance Warren — employee
Jesse Wilheit
Russell Worley
Mark Worscheh